THE UPANISHADS

Katha • Prashna • Mundaka

Other Titles by Sri M

The Little Guide to Greater Glory and a Happier Life

Wisdom of the Rishis:
The Three Upanishads: Ishavasya - Kena - Mandukya

Jewel in the Lotus: Deeper Aspects of Hinduism

How to Levitate and Other Secrets of Magic

The Upanishads - Katha, Prashna, Mundaka

Shunya: A Novel

On Meditation - Finding infinite Bliss & Power Within

The Journey Continues -

Sequel to Apprenticed to a Himalayan Master

Apprenticed to a Himalayan Master
A Yogi's Autobiography

The Autobiography of Sri M available in the following languages:
Hindi, Marathi, Tamil, Telugu, Kannada, Malayalam, Oriya, German, Russia, Bengali, Gujarati, Italian, Spanish

The Journey Continues available in the following languages:
Hindi, Marathi, Gujarati

To buy books and discourses by Sri. M online visit magentapress.in

THE UPANISHADS

Katha • Prashna • Mundaka

By

Sri M

Transcribed by

Uma Singh

Edited by

Roshan Ali

With a foreword by

Dr. Karan Singh

Magenta Press

Reprint : July 2017
Reprint : June 2019

ISBN: 978-81-95608-94-2
2022 edition

Book Design: J. Menon. www.grantha.com

Typeset: PKS

Published by Magenta Press and Publication Pvt. Ltd.
No.9,1st Floor,Websters Road, Cox Town, Bangalore - 560005. Karantaka, India
iv

Tel: +91 9343071537 / 6363083590. info@magentapress.in,www.magentapress.in

My Param Guru Sri Guru Babaji.

My Guru Sri Maheshwaranath Babaji.

Contents

Preface

The contents of this book are the edited transcriptions of the discourses on the Upanishads by Sri M.

Minimum editing has been done to retain the style of the talks. The editor acknowledges the contribution of Ms. Uma Singh in transcribing the discourses with care and attention.

The introductory portions might sound repetitious at times, but that could not be avoided, considering that the talks were given at different times to different people. It is suggested that these portions be re-read for a thorough comprehension of each Upanishad.

– Editor

Foreword

The Upanishads represent the high watermark not only of Hindu Philosophy but of spiritual literature anywhere in the world. These marvellous discourses and dialogues between self-realized seers, known as Rishis, and one or more disciples, contain powerful and eloquent statements regarding the ultimate reality in its multifarious facets. They have been well described as providing an 'ecstatic slide show of reality, a privileged glimpse of the unitive vision in which all thing are one in a world aflame with God'. They contain some of the most eloquent passages such as – 'I have seen that Great Being shining like a thousand suns beyond the darkness; it is only by knowing that being that we can achieve immortality' and again, 'Hear O children of immortal bliss, you are born to be united with the Divine; follow the path of the illumined ones and be united with the Supreme Being'.

The universal truths articulated in the Upanishads have formed the basis for numerous commentaries down through the centuries, beginning with the luminous insights of Adi Shankaracharya. In our own times Sri Aurobindo, Sri Krishnaprem, Dr Radhakrishnan, Swami Ranganathananda, Eknath Ishwaran and other great seers and sages have produced commentaries and interpretations on various Upanishads. The Upanishads are enduring and unfailing sources of inspiration, and their impact grows with each successive reading. One of my favourites is the *Mundaka* which I have translated and upon which I have attempted a short commentary.

The author of this book, Sri Mumtaz Ali, popularly known as 'M', has spoken extensively upon the Upanishads, based on his personal experience. The fact that a person born a Muslim should have such a deep insight into the Hindu tradition proves once again that the spiritual path accepts no boundaries.

In these talks M has expounded in a clear and cogent fashion various aspects of these three great texts. I have pleasure in commending this book to spiritual seekers and students of Hinduism around the world.

– Dr. Karan Singh

A Profile of 'M'

The boy was a little more than 9 years old when he saw the strange being. He was the son of a Deccani Muslim family, settled in Trivandrum, the beautiful capital of Kerala. Having heard stories of angels coming down to bless Mohammed and other prophets and saints from his devout grandmother, he thought at first that it was an angel.

One evening, the boy was wandering around the courtyard of his house in Vanchiyoor, doing nothing in particular. At the far end of the courtyard, he saw someone standing under the jackfruit tree. The stranger gestured to the boy to come forward. The boy felt no fear whatsoever, and was eager to go closer to the stranger.

The stranger was tall, fair and well-built and was bare-bodied except for a piece of loin cloth worn around his waist. He put his right hand on the boy's head and asked with kindness, "Do you remember anything?" in Hindi. To the boy's answer that he didn't, the stranger said in Deccani, "You will understand later. You will not meet me for many years after this, but you will have to finish the studies that you have left incomplete. You will not be allowed to tell anyone about me until the time is ripe. Go home now." With that he vanished.

That was the first initiation. Two years later, while playing hide and seek, the boy experienced what may be described in yogic terms as *Keval Kumbhak* – the suspension of inhalation and exhalation. Bliss filled his heart. The breathing resumed in a few minutes.

Soon he could get into it at will with a deep sigh. The bliss that he experienced convinced him that a greater world existed within his being – a world of spiritual bliss.

In his outward appearance he was just like any other boy except that he loved religious scriptures and philosophy – no matter of which religion, devotional songs and discussions on God, saints and sages.

When he was eleven, he used to go in the evenings to a certain house which belonged to one Mr. Pillai, whose nephew and son-in-law tutored him in mathematics. One evening he entered Pillai's house as usual and found himself face to face with a venerable, sturdy man of about sixty, clean shaven and with closely cropped silver grey hair, wearing a half sleeved shirt and loin cloth, sitting cross-legged on a bench. The room smelled of incense.

"Hello!" said the old man in Malayalam, "Come, come. Don't be afraid."

'M' walked up to him. The man patted his back and caressed his neck and head and said, "Umm. Good! Everything will be all right in good time."

Again the breathless condition and greater bliss. 'M' stood up and went straight home. The guidance had begun. He was the first of the great souls 'M' was to meet in the course of his spiritual journey.

Much later 'M' came to know that the man was a great self-realised soul who lived in 'Atma Bhava' and was simply called Pujapura Swami since he lived in Pujapura. He was unmarried but not a formal monk. In his youth he had been initiated into yogic practices by a great teacher and ever since had lived a model life, his heart absorbed in the blissful, Supreme Brahman while he performed his duties like an ordinary mortal.

'M' also learnt that the Swami used to hold midnight Satsangs on certain days, which a great sanyasin, who had renounced even his loin-cloth, would sometimes attend. Pujapura Swami was not known outside a small circle because he forbade propaganda.

When 'M' was seventeen, the *sanyasin* was no more, but a friend handed over a compilation of his teachings to 'M' which was privately circulated. It contained the essence of *Vedanta* in very simple language.

By then, the knowledge that 'M' needed from time to time as he progressed on the path began to come to him automatically. His father had borrowed B. K. S. Iyengar's *Light on Yoga* from a friend of his (his father was never an orthodox Muslim). 'M' read it through. A yoga teacher, Sri Sharma, gave him his initial lessons on yogasanas and Surya Namaskaras.

'M' met Swami Tapasyananda of the Ramakrishna Mission, a direct disciple of Sarada Devi. He was then the head of Ramakrishna Mission at Trivandrum. The librarian at the Trivandrum Public Library kept 'M' well supplied with the works of Vivekananda. He chanced to read Swami Chinmayananda's *Japa Yoga* and *Gayatri* and he began to chant the Gayatri Mantra. A Tantric instructed him in certain mantras and lent him Sir John Woodroffe's *Serpent Power*. He read many other books – the *Upanishads,* the *Gita,* Yogic texts and *Vedanta* included. He discovered that Sanskrit was not too difficult to understand.

Side by side with gaining theoretical knowledge, he meditated for long hours, especially at midnight. He had merely to shut his eyes and concentrate on the lotus of the heart to enter into Keval Kumbhak and experience tremendous bliss and extraordinary visions of divine lights and voices. Sometimes terrifying visions would flit across his mind but they would pass and he would once again be filled with ecstasy.

Then he met a great person known as Chempazanthi Swami. The Jesuits had started their first Loyola Junior College at Sreekaryam in Trivandrum and 'M' was among the first batch of pre degree students. A few kilometers away was the remote village of Chempazanthi which is the birth place of Sri Narayana Guru, the great reformer-saint. Close to Chempazanthi is Chenkotkonam where the Swami lived.

He was a tea-shop owner turned saint. A great *bhakta* of Rama, he was known to have lived like Hanuman for a long time, eating nuts and climbing trees. He was fond of bhajans and kirtans. When 'M' met him in his hut, he was thin and frail and very delicate looking. Crowning his ever-smiling face was a great chunk of wound-up matted hair and he smelled of Vibhuti. Taking a pinch of ash, he touched M's forehead with it, popped a couple of grapes into his mouth and said, 'Umm, needs to ripen, will ripen. Do bhajans.' 'M' meditated for a few minutes, prostrated and left the place.

Those days 'M' had a close Brahmin friend whose father worshipped Sai Baba of Shirdi. The moment 'M' saw Baba's picture , an irresistible desire to know about Baba's life rose in him. The next day Mr. Subramanya Iyer, an advocate, who was his friend's landlord, gave him a copy of the *Life of Sai Baba of Shirdi* by Narasimha Swamiji." Then he lent 'M' *Sai Sat Charita*. He fell in love with the great Faqir.

At this time 'M' heard from a friend of his who was a medical student (he is now a neuro-surgeon) about a lady Avadhuta called Mai Ma, who lived on the Kanyakumari beach. She was reputed to be over a hundred years old and no one could say where she came from or what language she spoke. The few words she said sounded very much like Bengali.

'M' went to see her alone. Kanyakumari is close to Trivandrum. He reached Kanyakumari a little before noon. He walked from the bus stand and came to the entrance of the Devi Temple. He casually walked across the rocky beach and there she was. A woman who looked to be in her sixties, she wore absolutely no clothes, her face a typically Bengali face, glowing, ageless eyes, smiling. She sat on one of the rocks with a circle of street dogs around her forming a security ring. The dogs snarled when they saw 'M.'

Mai Ma scolded the dogs using peculiar sounds and they dispersed and sat at a distance. She motioned to 'M' to sit down. He sat down on a rock. She pointed to the dosas that he had with him and said something. He gave her the dosas. She fed the dogs some, ate two herself and returned a few to him. He closed his eyes and tried to tune in with her vibrations. After a long time he opened his eyes. She was still there. Giving a broad smile she said, "*Jao, jao, thik*..." The last word could not be made out.

When Paramahamsas say "Go", one has no business to stay. 'M' prostrated and came away. After visiting the Vivekananda Rock, 'M' returned to Trivandrum.

He was made aware of the significance of Mai Ma's darshan the following morning. Tired after meditating for a long time in the night, he could not bring himself to be up at dawn. As he slept deeply he had a wonderful and vivid dream. In the dream he was a mendicant with matted hair and wearing only a 'kaupin,' sitting in padmasana and meditating under a Banyan tree which stood in the middle of a junction where four paths crossed each other. The jungle all around was thick.

A faint sound made him open his eyes, and from one of the paths he saw Mai approaching with a stick in her hand. She was huge, much larger than life-size. Reaching the place where he sat she touched his chin and said, "Give me something to eat."

He told her, "Mai Ma, I have only two grains of parched rice hidden in my matted hair."

She said, "Give me."

Without hesitation he gave the rice to her. She said to him, "Are you hungry?" He said "Yes, but you eat it Ma." She ate with great relish and turning to him said, "Your hunger is for a different thing. Close your eyes."

He closed his eyes. She pressed the middle of his forehead hard with what seemed to be her thumb. An ocean of bliss filled his whole being with its centre in the forehead. Every cell of his being was suffused with it. He lost his body consciousness. Only the other existed.

Then he woke up. The dream vanished, but O! How fortunate! The bliss remained. He was like a drunken man who had had his fill. Slowly he sat up and stretched his legs and carefully went to the bathroom, afraid that he would fall. In a few minutes he got full control over his body and mind but the stream of bliss continued in the core of his being. It has since remained with him. At times low, at times high, but always there.

Already acquainted with the teachings of the Sufis by attending meetings of local Sufi groups and meeting some of the Amirs of the different Tariqats, he went at last to a gem among Sufis.

That was Kaladi Mastan who lived naked on the beach near Bimapalli in Trivandrum. He was drinking a cup of tea given by a follower when 'M' first saw him. He smiled and gave 'M' the rest of the tea. Then he said, "Big thief came to steal the treasure. Take it legitimately." Then he lit a cigarette and said, "Smoke." 'M' smoked. Then he took it back. 'M' sat and meditated before him. He covered M's head with sand and further cleared the conduits. He behaved like a mad man and many even thought he was mad, but he was a priceless gem and the few who were serious, knew. He is physically no more now. Many visit his tomb.

Not very far from there lived Poontharasami, another God-intoxicated person with matted hair, who too was mistaken by many to be a madman. When 'M' visited him, he suddenly stood up and kicked 'M' on his chest. That was a timely kick. It cleared the passage through which the mighty energy travels.

When 'M' went to thank him a month later, he had vanished, nobody knew where. An impressive looking fraud, who claimed to have been his closest disciple, tried to influence 'M.' The poor chap did not realize that 'M' could read him like an open book.

When he was nineteen, 'M' made up his mind to go to the Himalayas. First he went to Madras by train, spent sometime in the Theosophical Society, then took a train to Delhi. From Delhi he went to Hardwar. From Hardwar he decided to walk.

All the money was finished. He had no intention of writing back home for help or even to let them know where he was. He knew he would be looked after, that the minimum needs of the body would be taken care of by the great powers that run the universe, and he was right. Of course, at certain times, he was tested thoroughly but in the end everything was fine. On foot he covered the entire journey from Rishikesh to Uttarkashi, to Gangotri, Yamunotri, from Batwari to Kedar via Buda Kedar, then to Badrinath.

At Rishikesh, he decided to stay in the Divine Life Society and continue his studies and meditation. It is a lovely place for *sadhaks*.

The Ganges flows nearby. Yoga is taught in the Ashram. The senior swamis are a great help and when one has time, one can wander around and meet sadhus of various sects. Satsang is most important for a sadhak.

That pilgrim-season found 'M' walking again to Badrinath – sometimes on the common pilgrim routes, sometimes through forests, staying in roadside *dharmashalas* and *chattis* and many a time in forest hermitages beside the river. On his way to Badrinath, he visited Vasishta Guha and Arundhati Cave. He gathered much food for the soul.

Reaching Badrinath after many days' journey, he first slept in the choultry. It was quite cold and his single blanket was insufficient, but he was in no mood to seek help. Those were the days when the fire of spirituality burned so bright that everything else, even the bare necessities – food, clothes and shelter – melted into insignificance. A highly intoxicating, ecstatic mood came over him in the great Himalayas. He attributed this, as also his intense sadhana to the presence of highly evolved beings in these regions. He hoped to meet some of them.

His physical difficulties were solved by the arrival of a Brahmachari whom he had met earlier in the Divine Life Society. He was an experienced pilgrim who had travelled many times. Quickly he found 'M' an independent kutir and persuaded him to stay there. He also got 'M' a couple of blankets and a wooden plank to sleep on; he also arranged with the Nepali Dharmashala for his food. He introduced 'M' to the Rawalji, the chief priest of Badrinath, and took him on a sort of conducted tour on most evenings.

In Badrinath as in other pilgrim centres, there were beggars wearing saffron, others wearing the holy robes to make a living, even sadhus who stole *kamandalus* and blankets from each other.

Genuine yogis and *paramahamsas* also existed side by side, mingling with the common crowd and often deliberately pretending to be one of them.

Eager to see more of such souls and learning that they lived beyond Badrinath and on the other side of Narayan Parvat, 'M' decided to travel further. Without informing anyone, one morning he started off with his *kamandalu*, staff and blanket.

He had earlier explored about a kilometer of that road on his previous visit to Badrinath but beyond that the territory was unknown. After about six or seven kilometres of not easy climbing, he reached the confluence of the Saraswati and the Alakananda, called Keshav Prayag. Close to this was the cave, which, an old sanyasin had once told him, was the Vyasa Guha.

'M' walked beyond the Vyasa Guha to explore the other caves in the vicinity. He had walked through the rocky terrain for a long time when he realized that it would soon grow dark. Filled with doubt, fear and hunger, and disappointed about not finding any *mahatmas*, 'M' began to walk down towards the Mana village. On the way back, when he reached the Vyasa Guha, he found that a *dhuni* was brightly burning at the mouth of the cave. A strange force seemed to make his feet heavy. His heart overflowed with bliss but his legs would not move away from the cave. He took this as a signal and walked towards the cave. From inside the cave came a voice calling him by the name "Madhu". Seeing this young man, the long-haired, bare-bodied, tall man patted on his left shoulder with great affection and asked him to sit. At that instant, 'M' recognised the person whom he had once met in the backyard of his house under the jackfruit tree. He had found his guru, his father, his mother, all in one.

'M' spent three and a half years with his Master travelling all over the Himalayas. The Master advised him to go back to the plains and lead a normal life and begin teaching when commanded to do so. The Master promised to keep in touch. The Master had thoroughly overhauled his thought-process and brought about a lasting change in his consciousness.*

According to the Master's advice, 'M' went back to the plains, met many spiritual teachers and godmen, travelled all over India, took up difficult jobs to earn a living and to "see the world at close quarters," as the Master put it. He also lived for a short while like a very materialistic-minded person, and found that compared to the spiritual life and its greater vistas, the life of the worldly man is almost nothing. The joys of the spirit are much superior and it is the worldly man who renounces real happiness that springs from the heart.

But all that experience was necessary to tackle the worldly-wise who would say, "Oh! what do you know of the bliss of sensory experiences. You have not had any."

Now 'M' feels that he can say with confidence, "Friend, I know, and there is nothing to go ga ga about."

Off and on he had attended the talks of J. Krishnamurti in Madras and elsewhere and read most of his literature. Finally he met him and had a private discussion for forty-minutes after which he decided to stay on in the Krishnamurti Foundation for sometime. The Master had said that Krishnamurti would be the last of the important persons that 'M' would meet as part of his education and had instructed him to pay particular attention to everything that 'K' did and how the organisation would function when he lived and after his death. 'M' had close contact with J. Krishnamurti during the last two years of his life and was made a Trustee of the Krishnamurti Foundation, which position he resigned after five years.

After K's death 'M' married Sunanda whom he had met in Vasant Vihar, the headquarters of the Krishnamurti Foundation, and became a householder.

He now feels that no one can say to him, "Well, brother, it is alright for you to say, 'lead a spiritual life and live in the world etc.', because you are unmarried..." and so on. 'M' lives with his wife and two children. "In fact, it is the best thing to do in this period of the earth's existence, for *Sanyasa* is only for the rarest of the rare," says 'M.' With the blessings of his Himalayan Master and by strenuous sadhana 'M' has transcended theories and scholarship and is established in higher consciousness.

The Master had said to 'M,' "Do not advise people if you cannot follow the same advice. Do not talk on something if you have no personal experience." Wonderful teaching indeed! If only teachers follow this teaching what a lovely world this would be!

– Gp. Capt. (Retd.) Ratnakar Sanadi

(For a detailed account of Sri M's life, please read his autobiography *Apprenticed to a Himalayan Master – A Yogi's Autobiography* and *The Journey Continues*, a sequel to the autobiography)

Katha Upanishad

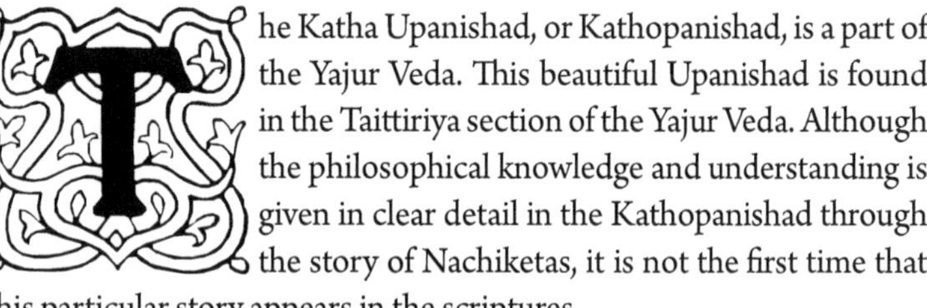

The Katha Upanishad, or Kathopanishad, is a part of the Yajur Veda. This beautiful Upanishad is found in the Taittiriya section of the Yajur Veda. Although the philosophical knowledge and understanding is given in clear detail in the Kathopanishad through the story of Nachiketas, it is not the first time that this particular story appears in the scriptures.

The earliest occurrence of the story of the boy Nachiketas, is in the Rig Veda, though not in detail. One can find the detailed version in the Taittiriya Brahmana. In fact, in the Anushasan Parva of the Mahabharat, there is a brief reference to it. Nachiketas questions his father, the great *rishi* Vaajashravasa, about a certain idea that occurs to him and then the entire Upanishad is about what happens subsequently.

It is a very old story, or *katha,* which has been utilized by this Upanishad so that one may understand the deeper aspects of "being". In the Upanishads, what is important is not the person who is talking or the person who is listening, but the teaching. Anyone can talk to anybody, but whether the one who is talking has knowledge, and whether the one who is listening is open to it – that is the main concern of the Upanishads.

As we go along, sometimes you will find some names interchanged. You will suddenly come across someone in this Upanishad being called by a name that is someone else's in some other Upanishad. So it is not the name that is important but the actual substance.

Let us first get an idea of what an Upanishad is and then come to the Kathopanishad. To sum up briefly, an Upanishad is what is known as the "Wisdom Section", the *jnaanakaanda* of the Vedas. Vedas include the *Samhitas,* the *Brahmanas,* the *Aranyakas* and the Upanishads. The Upanishad appears at the end of the Vedas, as the last part. Since it comes at the end of the Vedas, it is also called *veda-antah,* which means "the end of the Vedas". Some people have given a different meaning to this. It is said *veda* means "to study", "to read", "to understand" and Vedanta means "once this is understood, there is nothing more to be studied". Thus again, it means "end of the Vedas."

Apart from that, the word "Upanishad" is formed by the three syllables, *upa, ni* and *shad. Upa* means "to move closer" and *shad* means "to sit down". *Upa* – to move closer; not just the physical proximity but also to go closer and closer to the understanding of what is being said by the *rishis.* It also means moving closer to the Truth. Besides, the Upanishad is not something to be read – unfortunately, that is what we are doing now – but heard. The Upanishad is part of the literature which is known as the *shruthi* – "that which is heard." It is not something which we hear and then take with us, store it in the brain, go home, think about it and decide whether we want to understand it or not. Then it is not *shruthi* any more. If the mind is kept open, the moment it is said, it is understood. This is the *shruthi.*

The word *shad* means "to sit". When you sit down, you are settled and you want to listen to something. When you stand up, it means you are unsettled, you may want to walk out. So when you sit down, it means that physically, you have sat down to listen. It also means that the mind has settled down. Sometimes, physically one can sit here but the mind can wander. "Sit down" means the mind has to also sit down and listen.

The *ni* that connects *upa* and *shad* is the syllable that indicates the attitude with which one is sitting. *Ni* indicates that the person who is listening is sitting at a lower level. However, it means that the person who is listening is sitting, not physically, but with the attitude of "I have to understand." If I say, "I know," then I cannot understand. If I say, "I know," before examining something, then there is no examination. One cannot look into it. So I sit down saying, "For the time being, let me put aside the things that I know and let me listen to what is being said." When you want to pour liquid from one vessel to another, you have to keep the other vessel below. What it means is to have an open mind and the humility to say, "I don't know. Let me listen."

If the teacher has gone deep into the subject, he or she will also have the humility to say, "This is what I have understood: listen, and find out for yourself if it is true." The entire Upanishadic teaching is a dialogue. It is not as if somebody says, "You hear this and you believe it." No! It says, "Look into this. Follow instructions and find out for yourself and then decide what you want." This is how the Upanishad teaches.

The Katha Upanishad is one of the ten principal Upanishads. The great Adi Shankaracharya has also written a commentary on it. It is called *katha* because it is a story; it begins with a story. This Upanishad comes from the Yajur Veda and is one of the earlier Upanishads. Most of the Upanishads begin with an invocation. There is a meaningful invocation in this Upanishad, which is a very popular one, chanted in many schools and religious institutions. It is:

Aum saha naav avatu
saha nau bhunaktu
saha veeryam karavaavahai
tejasvi nav adheetam astu
maa vidvishaavahai
Aum shantih shantih shantih

"May that Supreme Being protect both of us;
May that Supreme Being be pleased with both of us;
May we both work together with vigour;
May our study make us both illumined;
Let there be no misunderstanding between us.
Aum peace! Peace! Peace!"

During the Upanishadic teaching, when the teacher and student sit down together, neither is more important than the other. The prayer is for them both: "May that Supreme Being protect both of us", "May He be pleased with both of us. May we work together with *veeryam* (vigour)."

One needs energy and vigour to do any work. This is one of the questions that Nachiketas asks his father, in the course of the Upanishad. He asks his father, who was gifting decrepit cows which had no strength, "Why are you giving away these feeble cows for sacrifice? There is nothing in them. Give away something that has energy."

"May we work together with energy and vitality. May our study and understanding make us illumined." The teacher says, "I am getting illumined by the teaching. So also is the student." This is mutual understanding and co-operation. Without such involvement, the Upanishad cannot be understood.

I say this because I go for talks and sometimes, a question is not asked as a question; it is more an argument. Or, someone tries to tell us what he knows, or we try to oppose him with what we think is right. The Upanishad cannot be studied that way.

It has to be studied with an understanding that the chief import of the Upanishad must be the search for the Truth. That is why in the Upanishads, the person who looks for the Truth is called *satya kaama*. In the Chandogya Upanishad, you will read about Satyakaama Jabala, whose name Satyakaama means he who has but one 'desire' or (*kaama*), which is to find the 'truth' (*satya*); nothing else is important to him.

Then: *Aum shantih shantih shantih* – "Aum Peace! Peace! Peace!" Ultimately, peace is what we need. If the study of the Upanishad does not bring peace, then it is better to wind up such a study. Ultimately whatever you have, if there is no peace, it means nothing.

So this *shantimantra* talks about the equal importance of the teacher as well as the student, or, the speaker as well as the listener and how both the teacher and the taught are to be protected and sustained. They have to work together to understand the Truth and there need be no dislike between the two. This is the essential message of the Upanishad.; It says, "Listen to what is being said, so that there is no disagreement between the two." The Upanishadic exercise is not one of argumentation but one of discussion and understanding.

All that have been stated here are not my words. I am only translating what has been said in the Upanishad, which is the *shruthi,* which is the original scripture of this ancient land;. We now begin the Katha Upanishad with a story.

Part 1: CHAPTER 1

SHLOKA 1

ushan ha vai vaajashravasah sarva vedasam dadau
tasya ha nachiketaa naama putra aasa

"The sage, Vaajashravasa, desirous of heaven, performed a sacrifice in which he gave away all his possessions. He had a son called Nachiketas."

The story goes that the sage Vaajashravasa desired heaven and for this he performed the Vishvajit sacrifice to win the entire universe. He gave away everything so that he could attain the *svarga loka* – "heaven". This is our usual behaviour. We are ready to give up everything as long as we achieve our aim in life. So Vaajashravasa was also ready to do that. Performing that sacrifice, he gave away all that he possessed.

He had a son called Nachiketas. The word *nachiketa* is interesting. It means "one who does not understand", and therefore wants to understand. But Vaajashravasa feels that he has understood everything: he knows what he wants to get and he is giving away everything for that. Here is the son, still young, and with an open mind who does not understand and therefore wants to understand the Truth.

The son watches his father giving everything away in sacrifice in order to attain *svarga loka.*

SHLOKA 2

tam ha kumaaram santam dakshinaasu niiyamaanaasu
shraddhaa vivesha sah manyata

"When the gifts were being given away to the priests, *shraddhaa* entered into the heart of the young boy, and he thought"

What does *shraddhaa* mean? It has been loosely translated as "faith". *shraddhaa* means all these things put together: faith in one's self, one-pointedness, total attention to the real as opposed to the unreal, to the true as opposed to the hypocritical. That *shraddhaa,* for understanding the Truth, entered the heart of the young boy Nachiketas.

Although he was just a boy, as he looked at the cows that were being given away as gifts to the priests who had come to conduct the sacrifice, a thought entered his mind:

SHLOKA 3

peetodakaa jagdha trinaa dugdha dohaa nirindriyaah
anandaa naama te lokaas taan sa gacchata taa dadat

"What joyless world will they go, who present such decrepit cows, whose water is drunk, who have eaten their grass, who have given their milk and will have no more calves?"

Nachiketas saw the decrepit cows that were being presented to the priests. They were so old and useless that their water was "drunk", meaning that all their body fluids had dried. They seemed to have "eaten their grass", meaning nothing more remained to be eaten. Their milk had been exhausted and there was no more strength left in their senses or *indriyas.* They had become useless.

Nachiketas wondered to what joyless world they would go, those who present such cows as a sacrifice. What joyous world or *svarga,* can one hope to reach when all one has to give is something that is spent and useless?

This means, when we have used all our energies for useless things and when all the energy has gone, if we want heaven, what do we have left to give? All has been spent, nothing is left. If one has nothing to give, what will one sacrifice?

When Swami Vivekananda was wandering around India as an unknown monk, he met a young man, who said to him, "I would like to give up everything and become like Gautama Buddha." Swamiji said that it was a wonderful idea and asked, "What is your education?" The young man said that he had never been to school. "What is your parentage?" The young man said that he was an orphan. "Do you have any property?" The young man replied that he had nothing at all. Swamiji asked, "Then what are you going to give up? The Buddha gave up his entire kingdom and became the Buddha. But you have nothing to give; so what will you give up?"

Nachiketas wondered, "Here is someone who is seeking immortality and heaven – *svarga loka* – where he can remain for ages in bliss, without fear of want, without hunger and thirst. Such a person is giving away useless things like old and frail cows." Cows here are only symbolic. It means that when everything has been spent and one thinks of going to the higher spheres, then there is nothing left to give to go there. The entire life is wasted.

Nachiketas could not keep quiet for it had entered his heart. He was compelled to speak to his father.

SHLOKA 4

sa hovaacha pitaram taata kasmai maam daasyaseeti
dviteeyam triteeyam tam hovaacha mrityave tva dadaameeti

"He said to his father, 'Father, whom will you give me to?' And he repeated this question for a second and third time. The father heard this and said, 'I will give you away to Death.'"

What Nachiketas meant to tell his father was that, whatever he was giving away was useless. For a real sacrifice, if he really wanted to get something, he would have to sacrifice something precious. And since he was his father's most precious possession, "Who will you give me to?" was his question.

The entire world is created in sacrifice. Physically, the father gives something away and the mother receives – it is a sacrifice. The mother goes through the sacrifice of suffering, before the child is born. Everything in this universe is the result of some sacrifice or the other.

Nachiketas realised this and so he said to his father, "I am the dearest to you – the other things are useless. Who will you give me away to in sacrifice?" And he asked not once, but repeated the question *dviteeyam triteeyam* – "twice, thrice."

The father heard this question repeated three times, and then he answered, "I will give you away to Death."

There have been various interpretations of this. Some explain this as to mean that the father was annoyed with the boy repeatedly asking him this serious question during the sacrifice and so he impatiently replied by saying, "I will give you away to Death." He was irritated: "This chit of a boy, what is he saying now? Is he asking me a serious question?" This is one interpretation.

The other explanation is that the father Vaajashravas, who was himself a great *rishi,* knew that there is only one thing by which one can begin to understand the impermanence of life, and that was death. Whatever we do, however much we gather, one day we have to go and death has to take us.

So he told the boy, "I give you away to Death." The *rishi* meant this to be the final test: "Find out for yourself now: if you know Death, then you know the entire universe, the whole wisdom of existence. So, I give you away to Death." That means if you are dead to the universe, you are born to the spirit. Death does not mean that you run away from the earth.

There is a beautiful statement in the New Testament: "He who loseth his life shall gain it. He who gaineth his life shall lose it." Looking comparatively at the significance of both one has to decide what is the most important.

Hearing his father's words, Nachiketas says to himself:

SHLOKA 5

bahoonaam emi prathamah bahoonaam emi madhyamah
kim svid yamasya kartavyam yan mayaadya karishyati

"Many have gone before me to Death and many will follow me. I go as the middling. What duty towards Yama has my father that he will accomplish through me?"

Nachiketas, though a young boy, thought about death as nothing peculiar. "Everybody has to die and I too am going to die. I am in the middle because so many have gone before me to death; so many more will follow me to death. I go as the middling."

He wondered what duty his father would accomplish by sending him away to Death. Then he continues to think about life, death and rebirth:

SHLOKA 6

anupashya yathaa poorve pratipashya tathaapare
sasyam iva martyah pachyate sasyam iva jaayate punah

"It was the same with my forefathers; it was the same also with men who come later. Just like corn, a mortal ripens, falls and is born again."

First the corn is green, then it ripens, then the seeds fall and new corn is born. This goes on eternally. Later, one decays and is reborn and the whole cycle is repeated. Nachiketas does not at all doubt the existence of life after death. He knows that like corn, one has to be born again.

That is not the central concern of the Upanishad. He knows that after death, although one is gone, one is reborn.

Thinking about all this, Nachiketas goes to Yama Loka, the Realm of Death. As the story goes, when Nachiketas enters Yama's world, Yama is away. Nachiketas waits there for three days, without food, for Yama to return.

How did Nachiketas enter the House of Death? He did not enter like an ordinary person, crying and weeping and fearing that he had to leave the earth behind. He entered like fire. He went with the intention of studying what death is. He had not gone there because he was compelled to go, he had not gone fearing what would happen on the other side, nor had he gone with any desire left behind.

We think that we are afraid of death because we are afraid of the unknown. But our fear of death is because we are afraid of leaving what is known. If we were promised that we could take everything that we have with us and die, nobody would be afraid. It would be wonderful, like a nice trip to Singapore and back. But we cannot do that.

There is a famous story of Guru Nanak and a Nawab Sahib, who was a miser, who would never give any money to charity. One day, Guru Nanak sent him a note with a sewing needle, saying, "Nawab Sahib, greetings! Please keep this needle safe with you. You are going to die and I am also going to die. When I come there and meet you, please give back the needle to me." The Nawab Sahib got quite worried. He thought, "How can I take this needle there and then give it to him when he comes?" So he said to Guru Nanak, "I cannot do this, Sir. I cannot take this needle there." Guru Nanak said, "Then how are you going to take all your wealth? Use it for the needy here in this world."

One of the greatest fears of death is that all the so-called near and dear things will be gone.

But Nachiketas did not go to the House of Death with such fears. He went with the intention of understanding the Truth. With vigour he entered the House of Death. But, as Yama was away, he waited for him outside his house, refusing all hospitality. After three days, Yama returned and was surprised to find this boy there.

Yama is told about the arrival of the boy. How?

SHLOKA 7

vaishvaanarah pravishaty atithir braahmano grihaan
tasyaitaam shaantim kurvanti hara vaivasvatodakam

"Like the universal fire, this *braahmana* guest entered into the house. He was offered the peace-offering of water, O son of Vaivasvaan."

Braahmana comes from the word *brahman*. Here it means *brahma vid brahmaiva bhavati* – "*Braahmana* is one who tries to understand the Supreme Brahman."

When this young *braahmana* guest entered, shining like fire, he was given respect and the peace offering of water. But Yama was not there to do that himself. So Nachiketas, whose desire was to know the

Truth, refused everything and waited without food and water for three days for Yama to arrive.

It is said that when a *braahmana,* a person who is searching for Brahman, the Truth, shining with energy, with the desire for Truth and only the Truth, enters your house, respect him and look after him. First give him water to wash his feet and water to drink and then feed him. If he remains unfed in your house and you do not look after him, then:

SHLOKA 8

aashaa prateekshe sangatam soonrutaam
cha ishthaa poorte putra pashunsh cha sarvaan
etad vrinkte purushasya alpamedhaso
yasya annashnan vasati braahmano grihe

"Hopes and expectations, friendship and joy, sacrifices and good works, sons and cattle – all are taken away from the man of poor intellect, in whose house such a *braahmana* enters and remains unfed."

Everything is taken away from a host who does not welcome a *braahmana* into his house and feed him and look after him. Such a person is referred to as *alpa medha* – "the one who has very poor intellect and limited understanding," as he does not respect the seeker of Truth.

Yama comes to Nachiketas, who was sitting outside his house and says to him:

SHLOKA 9

tisro raatreer yaad avatseer grihe
mey annashnan brahman atitthir namasyah
namaste astu brahman svasti mey astu
tasmaat prati treen varaan vrunneeshva

"O Braahmana, I bow down before you, respected guest. You have waited for three nights outside my house without food. Obeisance to you, O seeker of the Truth, and welfare be to me. For each of the three nights, therefore, choose three boons."

Here Death himself is welcoming Nachiketas as an honourable guest. That means, when there is such a seeker who is seeking nothing but the Truth, even Death respects him and is afraid of him.

The calm Nachiketas asks for the first boon from Yama:

SHLOKA 10

shaanta sankalpah sumanaa yathaa syaad
veetahmanyur gautamo maabhi mrityo
tvat prasrushtam ma abhivadet prateeta
etat trayaanaam prathamam varam vrinney

"May my father, Gautama, be without any anxiety.With his anger gone, may he be gracious to me, O Death. May he recognize me and greet me, when you send me back from here. This is the first of the three boons I choose."

Nachiketas asks Yama for the first boon, that his father Gautama should greet him without anger and recognize him when he returns. Here, the name "Gautama" is also used to refer to Nachiketas' father. Earlier, his father's name is mentioned as "Vaajashravasa". In the Upanishads, names are interchangeable. "Gautama" occurs in many other Upanishads, as in the Chandogya Upanishad, where there is a Gautama, who is the son of Haridrumat and the *guru* of Satyakama Jabala.

There appears the beautiful story of Satyakama Jabala, a young boy, like Nachiketas, whose only desire was to find the Truth,*satya*. He did not know who his father was. He said to his mother, Jabala, "Mother, I want to go to a teacher and learn about the Truth, the Brahman. But when I go there, I will be asked my parentage. I do not know who my father is. What shall I tell them?"

Jabala, his mother, said, "Look, before you were born, I worked as a maid in many places with various people. So I do not know who your father is. So go there and tell them the truth. A *braahmana* is judged by his truthfulness. Tell the teacher the truth. Say, 'This is what my mother told me; my name is Satyakama and I am the son of Jabala. So I am known as Satyakama Jabala.' That is enough."

The boy went to the great *rishi* Gautama, who was the son of Haridrumat, and said, "Sir, I have come to learn the Truth." The *rishi* asked him, "Who are you?" The boy replied, "I am Satyakama, the son of Jabala." He then told the story about his parentage and about his earnest desire to know about the Truth.

Gautama *rishi* said, "None but a seeker of Truth would have told me the truth without any pretensions. Therefore you are a perfect candidate for learning the Truth and I will teach you."

Here, Nachiketas asks Yama that his father Gautama should greet him without anger and that he should "recognize" him when he returns home.

This not only applies to the father in the story, but to others as well. Many times, the person who has found the Truth and gone back is not recognised. After finding the truth one is different; one is not the same person again. Not only do people not "recognize" that person but instead of welcoming him with happiness and joy, they may persecute him. Many people who have found the Truth have been persecuted. So it is a genuine request that Nachiketas makes.

In fact, in the New Testament it is said, "No prophet is welcome in his own place." What troubles the great man Jesus went through and hung on the cross just because He had seen the Truth! It need not be that one is hung on a wooden cross. But, that "crucifixion" generally takes place because the person who has seen the Truth is looking at things from a different dimension, which everyone cannot follow. So instead of saying, "I cannot see that angle", you dismiss it as either insanity or unacceptable. The plain fact is, you do not see that angle.

Also, it is a little difficult to adapt after seeing That. Suppose you have been living in darkness for many years and suddenly you see the sun in its full brightness; then, when you look down on the earth, you cannot see clearly for a long time because your eyes are dazzled by the brilliance of the Sun. It takes some time to adjust. So Nachiketas is asking for all these "adjustments".

Yama tells him not to worry. He says:

SHLOKA 11

yathaa purastaad bhavitaa prateeta
auddhaalakir aarunir mat prasrshtah
sukham ratrih shayitaa veeta manyus
tvaam dadrishivaan mrityu mukhaat pramuktam

"Through my favour, he will also recognize you, as of old, in the same way as Uddhalaka recognized his son Aruni. Seeing that you have been released from the jaws of Death, no more will he have any anger left and he will sleep peacefully through the nights."

Here again, is a name from another Upanishad: Uddhalaka, the great *rishi,* and his son Aruni are mentioned in the Chandogya Upanishad. Names are interchangeable in the Upanishads. What was till now "Nachiketas" is now being addressed as "Uddhalaka Aruni"- Aruni, the son of Uddhalaka.

"Released from the jaws of Death" – *mrutyumukhaat pramuktam* – does not mean that since he has come back from Yama, therefore, he has been "released from the jaws of Death". What Yama means is, "When you go back from here, you will be free forever from death," which means, "no more will death frighten you for you will understand what is real life and what is immortality." Therefore, you are "released from the jaws of Death."

Then Nachiketas asks about the world of heaven:

SHLOKA 12

svarge loke na bhayam kin cha naasti
na tatra tvam na jaraya bibheti
ubhe teertva ashanaayaa pipaase
shokaatigo modate svargaloke

"In the world of heaven, there is no fear whatsoever. You, Death, also do not go there and there is no fear of old age. There is no hunger and there is no thirst and therefore, leaving sorrow behind, one rejoices in the world of heaven."

Nachiketas is talking to Yama about the "world of heaven" – *svarga loka* – "where one rejoices as there is no fear that Death will come and take us away; where one is free from old age, hunger and thirst and so, there is no sorrow." In that world, there is nothing to fear whatsoever because you will never grow old and you will remain young. There is no fear of old age, death, catastrophes or cyclones. One enjoys a relatively long life.

When Nachiketas talks about the "world of heaven," *svarga loka,* he is not talking about the ultimate discovery of Truth, which is known as *moksha.* There is a difference. In asking for the second boon, he wants to know about heaven and in asking the third boon, he wants to know what is beyond *svarga* and what the ultimate Truth is.

Nachiketas asks for the second boon:

SHLOKA 13

sa tvam agnim svargyam adhyeshi mrityo
prabroohi tam shraddha daanaaya mahyam
svarga lokaa amritatvam bhajanta
etad dviteeyena vrinney varenna

"O Death, you know that fire-sacrifice, which is an aid to heaven Please describe it to me as I am full of faith. Tell me that secret by which one can gain immortality in heaven. This, I choose as my second boon."

As his second boon, Nachiketas asks Yama to tell him about that secret of the fire-sacrifice, that technique of reaching *svarga loka,* where there is no fear of old age or of death, where one lives for ages, rejoicing in happiness.

In the Vedas, everything that needs to be burnt, which needs energy, which needs light, is referred to as *agnim,* "fire". So "Tell me that *agnim* which will take me to *svarga.* This I choose as my second boon."

Yama replies:

SHLOKA 14

pra te braveemi tad u me nibodha
svargyam agnim nachiketah prajaanan
ananta lokaaptim atho pratishthaam viddhi
tvam etam nihitam guhaayaam

"I know that fire which will take you to heaven. I will describe it to you. You learn it from me, O Nachiketas. That fire is the means to attaining the boundless world of heaven. It supports the entire universe and resides in a secret place within you."

All the *acharyas* have interpreted "fire" as "desire". That is the fire of the desire for Truth. It is the same fire which is also the desire for happiness.

What is this desire that keeps us evolving, keeps us moving in this world? It is the desire for happiness and it is like a fire that burns in us all the time. While it is burning, it is wonderful; when it has finished burning, it becomes ash. It is this same fire which is also the search for the Supreme Being. The difference is, here it burns up and there, it burns down!

That fire resides in a secret place within the heart. "Heart" does not mean the physical heart; it means the "centre of one's consciousness".

In the next *shloka,* Yama describes that fire:

SHLOKA 15

lokaadim agnim tam uvaacha tasmai
yaa ishtakaa yaavateer vaa yathaa vaa
sa cha api tat pratyavadat yathoktam
atha asya mrityuh punar evaaha tushtah

"That fire-sacrifice, which is the source of the world, I will describe to you: what kind of bricks to use, how many, and, in what manner to place them and how to light the fire. Nachiketas then repeated it all, just as it had been told to him. Pleased with this, Death then said…"

Here, when Yama talks about the "bricks' to be used for the fire-sacrifice, he means the "building blocks" that will take one to *svarga loka.* When he says "fire", he means "desire".

When Yama mentions the "bricks", it is not as if he is going to describe how to arrange the bricks and light the fire. That is the external part of it. The Upanishad does not deal with the external part and the ceremonies – the *Brahmanas* deal with that.

So Yama said, "I will teach you that fire-sacrifice." He described it to him and taught him how to reach *svarga loka.* Nachiketas understood clearly what was taught and repeated it exactly as it was told to him. Death was delighted. Being so pleased, Death gave him an additional boon:

SHLOKA 16

tam abraveet preeyamaanno mahaatmaa
varam tava iha aadhya dadaami bhooyah
tava eva naamnaa bhavitaayam agnih
srinkaam cha imaam aneka roopaam gruhaanna

"The great Death was extremely delighted and he said to Nachiketas, 'I am giving you an additional boon. From now on, this fire-sacrifice will be named after you. Also, take this splendid chain of many shapes.'"

This "chain," *srinkaam,* has many interpretations. The various shapes and splendid beads that form the chain are meant to be all the blessings that one gets in *svarga loka.* All the blessings are put together in one chain. But, "chain" also means "that which binds". Chains can be made of iron, or silver or gold, but they are chains – "that which bind". So when Yama tells Nachiketas to take that splendid chain as an additional boon, he means, "Along with *svarga,* I give you all the joys that bind you. Take that too!"

Then Yama describes what happens to the one who performs the "Nachiketas fire" thrice. He says:

SHLOKA 17

trinnaachiketas tribhir etya sandhim
trikarma krut tarati janma mrityuu
brahmajajnnam devam iiddyam viditvaa
nichaayye maam shantim atyantam eti

"He, who has lit the Nachiketas fire thrice, associating with the three, having performed the three acts, crosses over birth and death. And knowing the Son of Brahman, the omniscient, the resplendent and adorable Agni, and realizing Him, he attains everlasting peace."

There are a few terms that have to be explained here. "He, who has lit the Nachiketas fire thrice", refers to the seeker who has understood "that" fire: he knows that in the inner being, fire of desire, of wanting to attain immortality, burns strong. He has lit the fire already and he has lit the fire thrice.

"Thrice" has different meanings. Basically, it means that not only has the fire been lit by the three dimensions of his being – the mind, speech and action (*manasa, vaacha, karmana*) – but they also reflect the seriousness with which he has lit that fire, which is the fire of desire to reach immortality.

"Associating with the three": these three are *shravana, manana and nidhidyasa,* which mean, not only listening to what is being said but thinking about it constantly, contemplating on it and understanding it.

"Having performed the three acts": there are three important acts or duties to be performed by a seeker or *sadhaka.* One is *ijja* or sacrifice, which means, unless you are ready to sacrifice something, you cannot get something higher. You cannot say, "I will do something, but everything will stay with me." Something has to go for something else to come in. There needs to be space. The second important act, *adhyayam* or study, is required. The third is *daana* or gifting. If you have both deep study and a sacrificing approach, involuntarily *daana* comes in, since you give away what is good for others, not only material goods but also the knowledge that you possess. The greatest *daana* is to give knowledge free.

So when a seeker lives performing the three acts, associating with the three and having lit the Nachiketas fire thrice, he crosses over birth and death. Knowing the Son of Brahman, he attains everlasting peace.

Here it says, "Son of Brahman, Agni", and not "Brahman the Supreme Being". By knowing the Son of Brahman, one attains *svarga loka* or heaven, which is the aim of the seeker who wants to attain this eternal world, where old age does not touch you and where there is much bliss and happiness. But it is not the Absolute Brahman, the Supreme Being, which the Upanishad is really seeking. The Upanishadic aim is to seek that Supreme Being, not just this *svarga*. But then, one cannot jump directly – most people would like to know what this is, and then proceed to the next step.

So this boon is for attaining *svarga loka,* which is considered to be one step lower than the Brahman.

In the Absolute state of Brahman, which is beyond the *svarga loka* mentioned here, the individual does not exist anymore. There is only the Supreme Being. The ego has been completely erased. Here, in *svarga,* the ego persists, enjoying itself as an individual. That is the difference.

So, the seeker, who has understood the Nachiketas fire, reaches that world of heaven, *svarga loka.* Then Yama says:

SHLOKA 18

trin naachiketas trayam etad viditvaa
ya evam vidvaams chinute naachiketam
mrityu paashaan puratah pranodya
shokaatigo modate svargaloke

"The wise man, who has in this manner, sacrificed thrice to the Nachiketas fire, who has known these three and thus knowing, throws off the bonds of death and overcoming sorrow, rejoices in the World of Heaven."

This is an Upanishad in *sutra* form, so one has to look into the commentaries. The wise man who has lit the Nachiketas fire thrice and has understood the "three", purifies himself in meditation, not only in the physical body, but also in the subtler levels of consciousness. So the wise man is purified in the physical body the *sthula sharira;* in the subtle body, the *sukshma sharira,* and in the subtlest body, the *karana sharira.* (I am deliberately not using the word "astral" because it is a very popular word nowadays: every other person fancies himself to be flying around in his astral body).

Such a wise man who purifies himself in meditation, not only in the physical body but also in the subtler levels of consciousness, "throws off the bonds of death, and overcoming sorrow, he rejoices in the world of heaven, in *svarga loka.*" But still, he remains in *svarga* not reaching beyond.

Yama then asks Nachiketas to choose his third boon. He says:

SHLOKA 19

esha teh agnir nachiketas svargyo
yam avrineethaah dviteeyena varena
etam agnim tava iva pravakshyanti janaasas
triteeyam varam nachiketo vrineeshva

"This is your fire, O Nachiketas, which leads to Heaven. You have chosen to know about this as your second boon. People will always call this fire-sacrifice by your name. Now choose your third boon."

As his third boon, Nachiketas asks Yama to clarify a doubt:

SHLOKA 20

yeyam prete vichikitsaa manushye
asti iti eke naayam asti iti cha eke
etat vidyaam anushishtas tvayaaham
varaanaam esha varas triteeyah

"There is this doubt – some people say that a person who has departed continues to exist somewhere. Others say he does not. I would like to know this from you. Please tell me. This is the third boon that I ask."

You must remember that Nachiketas has no doubt that the soul exists after leaving the body. That is not his question as he has previously said, "Just as corn ripens and falls and then corn is born again, so too a person is reborn, again and again." What he stresses upon here is "the free" when he says *prete* or "the departed."It is also the meaning that both Shankaracharya and Madhvacharya state in their interpretation, though otherwise, they are poles apart. But when they interpret this, Madhvacharya substitutes the word "the free" or *mukte* for *prete* and Shankara also says that here *prete* means *mukte.*

What Nachiketas wants to know is: What happens to a person when he is free? When one has attained spiritual freedom, when one is free from the surroundings, when one is free from the conditionings of this world, then what happens to one? Does one exist or not? Which means, is there only that Supreme Being in all its majesty? Or, is there also one little self inside enjoying It, or is the self merged with it? What is the Truth?

When Yama hears the question, he knows the seriousness of it. This question has been discussed not only in Hindu philosophy, but in various others; whether the state of freedom is one in which there is an individual or only the Supreme Consciousness.

In the Upanishadic way of teaching, it is never said, "It is like this, so you believe it!" The Upanishad always guides step by step, saying, "You look into this, you experience it and you find out what it is because of the simple fact that the Truth is not something which is like a material object." The Upanishad enquires into the Supreme Truth, the Brahman, which is not something material, which can be put into a test tube and given to us, like say, you put two compounds together and get a third. You cannot do that. We are talking about consciousness, which is immaterial.

Suppose Yama says, "Look! This is what happens – you actually exist" or "you do not exist – you are merged with Brahman", Nachiketas, who wants to know for himself, may not accept it. He has already challenged his father, the *rishi* Vaajashravasa, over the sacrifice. He would say, "You may say so but why should I believe it?" Hence, Yama leads Nachiketas, step by step, to an actual understanding of what it is. Here, the teacher is Yama; in the other Upanishads, it is other teachers who lead the students gradually, saying, "You understand what it is; and then you will find your answer to it. If I say something, it is my answer; it may not be yours." This is a very important part of the Upanishadic teaching.

So instead of directly listing and saying, "Yes, this is how you exist after death," and so on, Yama thought to himself, "I want to first find out if this fellow is really serious, or if he is trying to ask me for the sake of argument." There are many people who ask this question. But if you give them the same tests which Yama gave Nachiketas, they would rather agree and not question. They will say, "Ah! This is enough! I am happy. Who is bothered about what happens after death?" So Yama wants to test Nachiketas and find out if he is really serious about this question. Or, is he one of those who want to just say, "Oh! I have challenged even Death and asked him a question, which he could not answer."

Yama wants to find out how serious Nachiketas is. Is his interest, really, in finding the Truth alone? Or, is his interest in finding his own way of happiness in the name of Truth? Or, is he looking for entertainment, thinking that it is the Truth? This is the serious thing.

To find out how serious he is, Yama says to Nachiketas:

SHLOKA 21

devair atra api vichikitsitam puraa
na hi suvijneyam anur esha dharmah
anyam varam nachiketo vrinishva
maa ma uparotsir ati maa srijainam

"Even the gods of ancient times had some doubts about this point. It is not easy to understand. It is as subtle as the atom. So choose another boon, O Nachiketas. Do not compel me! Please release me from this problem."

Yama discourages him because he also wants to find out how strong and clear Nachiketas is on wanting to know the Truth.

Later on, Yama offers him various things to tempt him. He says, "Take all these things and be happy." Why do you want to ask this? Why do you want to get into all this? But Nachiketas says, "No! I do not want anything." How many people are there, who will not accept all that Yama offers, and remain really serious in their search for the Truth? Most will say, "If you are giving me all this, it is enough – forget about the Truth!"

In response to Yama's plea to not ask him that question and to ask for anything else, Nachiketas replies:

SHLOKA 22

devair atra api vichikitsitam kila
tvam cha mrityo yan na suvijneyam aattha
vaktaa cha asya tvaadrig anyo na labhyah
naanyo varas tulya etasya kashchit

"Even the gods had doubts about this, O Death, and you say it is not easy to understand. It is not easy to get a teacher like you on this subject. So I believe no other boon is equal to this."

Yama then tries another technique to discourage him. Actually, it is not that Yama does not want to go into this question. He wants to find out how serious this young boy really is. Yama says:

SHLOKA 23

shataayushah putra pautraan vrinishva
bahoon pashoon hasti hiranyam ashvaan
bhoomer mahad aayatanam vrineeshva
svayam cha jeeva sharado yaavad icchasi

"Choose sons, grandsons, who will live a hundred years; choose cattle in plenty, elephants, gold, horses; choose vast expanse of land

and yourself live as long as you want." In those days, cattle meant wealth.

Yama continues to offer more to Nachiketas:

SHLOKA 24

etat tulyam yadi manyase varam
vrinishva vittam chira jeevikaam cha
mahaa bhoomau nachiketas tvam edhi
kaamaanaam tvaa kaamabhaajam karomi

"If you think of any other boon equal to this, ask. Choose also wealth and long life, O Nachiketas. Prosper on this vast earth. I will make you the enjoyer of all desires. Choose!"

Yama continues to tempt Nachiketas:

SHLOKA 25

ye ye kaamaa durlabhaa martyaloke
sarvaan kaamaams chandatah praarthayasva
imaa raamaah sarathaah satooryaah
na hiidrushaa lambhaneeyaa manushyaih
aabhir mat prattaabhih parichaarayasva
nachiketo marannam ma anupraaksheeh

"Whatever desires are hard to attain in this world of mortals, ask for them, as you will. There are noble maidens with chariots and musical instruments, the like of whom cannot be won by men. Be served by them, whom I give to you. But Nachiketas, do not ask me about death."

This is the test for Nachiketas. He is saying, "I want to know about death and beyond death. I want to find the Truth." And here is Yama saying, "Please take these lovely maidens with their chariots and musical instruments; they will sing and also dance for you!"

But, Nachiketas is not impressed. He says to Yama:

SHLOKA 26

shvobhaavaa martyasya yad antakaitat
sarva indriyaanaam jarayanti tejah
api sarvam jeevitam alpam eva
tavaiva vaahaas tava nritya geete

"All these are transient, O Death. They wear out the vigour of all the senses in man. And the whole span of life is but short. So, keep the horses, song, and dance, for yourself." He continues:

SHLOKA 27

na vittena tarpaneeyo manushyah
lapsyaamahe vittam adraakshma chet tvaa
jeevishyaamo yaavad eeshishyasi tvam
varas tu me varaneeyah sa eva

"Man never gets contented with wealth. Having seen you, shall we enjoy wealth? Shall we live as long as you rule? That alone is the boon chosen by me."

Nachiketas says sensual pleasures are ephemeral and there is no point in asking for them. He says:

SHLOKA 28

ajeeryataam amritaanaam upetya
jeeryan martyah kvadhasthah prajaanan
abhidhyaayan varnnah ratih pramodaan
ati deerghe jeevite ko rameta

"Having approached the imperishable, undecaying immortal one, what decaying mortal being who knows he can receive more worthy boons from him, can exult in living long, after scrutinising the enjoyments of singing and dancing?"

Nachiketas makes it clear that he has no interest in these things:

SHLOKA 29

yasminn idam vichikitsanti mrityo
yat saamparaaye mahati broohi nas tat
yah ayam varo gooddham anupravishto
naanyam tasmaan nachiketaa vrinneete

"Tell us that, about which they have a doubt, O Death, what there is in that great passing on, after death. This boon, which penetrates that mystery, and no other than that does Nachiketas choose."

Nachiketas asks Yama for the answer to that mystery, about life after death, about which there is a doubt.

Yama is now convinced that the boy is indeed ardent about finding the Truth. Everything had been offered to him by the Lord of Death Himself and he knew that it would come through, if he accepted it. Yet, he said, "I want nothing else. I only want to know about The Truth."

Yama feels sure that Nachiketas is qualified to ask the question and he begins the teaching. He does not say, "This is what I say." The Upanishad does not directly say, "Yes, you exist," or, "you do not exist." It starts from the root of the problem and then guides you to discover the answer for yourself.

CHAPTER 2

Yama begins to teach the pure-minded and qualified student Nachiketas and goes to the root of the enquiry. Yama says to him:

SHLOKA 1

anyat shreyo anyad uta eva preyah
te ubhe naanaarthe purusham sineetah
tayoh shreya aadadaanasya
saadhu bhavati hee yate arthaad ya u preyo vrinneete

"Understand this: different is 'the good' and different indeed is 'the pleasant'. These two, with different purposes, bind a man. Both appear to a person. It is well for him who chooses 'the good' but he who chooses 'the pleasant' loses his goal."

Yama tells Nachiketas, "First understand the root of your enquiry, the beginning of your enquiry; that 'the good' is different from 'the pleasant'. What appears pleasant may not be good and what is good may not always be pleasant. So first understand this difference clearly. These two, 'the good' and 'the pleasant', bind a man for different purposes. Man comes face to face with 'the good' and also with 'the pleasant'. Both these come to a person. Of these two, it is well for him, who takes hold of 'the good' as he moves towards the goal. He who chooses 'the pleasant' loses his goal."

A serious seeker of the Truth must understand that there is a difference between "the good" and "the pleasant". Both appear to a person, a seeker, with their own purpose and bind man. A seeker who holds onto "the good" not worrying about whether it is pleasant or not, moves towards the goal. The person who chooses "the pleasant" over "the good", falls and misses his aim.

Yama tells Nachiketas the importance of choice:

SHLOKA 2

shreyas cha preyas cha manushyam etas
tau sampareetya vivinakti dheerah
shreyo hi dheeroh abhi preyaso vrineete
preyo mando yogakshemaad vrineete

"Both 'the good' and 'the pleasant' approach a person. The wise man ponders over them and distinguishes. The wise man chooses 'the good' in preference to 'the pleasant'. The other, for the sake of worldly well-being, chooses 'the pleasant'."

Both "the good" and "the pleasant" approach a person: what does he choose? This is the beginning of spiritual enquiry. The one, who misses "the pleasant" and takes up "the good", reaches the goal, if he seriously is a spiritual seeker of the Truth. The other, who is only happy with "the pleasant" – it does not matter what it is, whether good or bad – does not attain the aim of his search and misses the goal.

Yama praises Nachiketas' sense of discretion:

SHLOKA 3

sa tvam priyaan priyaroopaamscha kaamaan
abhidhyaayan nachiketo tyasraaksheeh
naitaam srunkaam vittamayeem avaapto
yasyaam majjanti bahavo manushyaah

"Therefore O Nachiketas, after examining them, you have rejected those desirable objects, which appear pleasant. You have not taken the path of wealth, where many mortals sink into ruin."

Yama says to Nachiketas: "You have rejected 'the pleasant', after examining it and you want to hold on to 'the good'. After discriminating, you have chosen wisely, the path of 'the good'. You have not chosen that path of wealth and possessions, which takes many men to ruin."He has not got into that which, the more it multiplies, the more you want. There is never an end to wanting more and more wealth and possessions. It is an unending act. At every level, somebody thinks he has less than the other.

Yama tells Nachiketas where the paths lead:

SHLOKA 4

dooram ete vipareete vishoochi
avidyaa yaa cha vidyeti inaataa
vidyaabheepsinam nachiketasam manye
na tvaa kaamaa bahavo lolupantah

"Widely apart and leading to divergent ends, are these two – 'ignorance' and what is known as 'wisdom'. You have chosen wisdom, Nachiketas, even the many desirable objects, which I set forth before you, did not distract you."

Yama considers Nachiketas as an aspirant for knowledge on his way to understanding. He warns him about "fools who think they are wise".

In the Mundaka Upanishad, you will find the popular saying "like the blind leading the blind." That was said at least three thousand years ago. Here is something, which Yama says a little differently.

SHLOKA 5

avidyaayam antare vartamaanaah
svayam dheerah panditam manyamaanaah
dandramya maannaah pariyanti mooddhah
andhenaiva neeyamaanaa yatha andhaah

"Abiding in the midst of ignorance, thinking that they are wise; and in their own esteem, thinking themselves to be learned; fools, treading a tortuous path, go about like blind men, led by one who is himself blind."

"Abiding in the midst of ignorance"- since this is said after Nachiketas has rejected everything but the desire to find the Truth, "ignorance" means "any desire to know that which is other than the Truth". So however learned we think we are, if the search for the Supreme Ultimate Truth is not our true desire, then we are more satisfied with "the pleasant" rather than "the good." Thus, he says, "They are like 'the blind leading the blind.'"

Yama talks about the fate of the deluded. He says:

SHLOKA 6

na saamparaayah pratibhaati baalam
pramaadhyantam vitta mohena mooddham
ayam loko naasti para iti maanee
punah punar vasham apadhyate me

"What lies beyond the attractions of the senses shines not to the ones who are simple-minded, careless and deluded by the glamour of worldly possessions. Thinking that this world alone exists and that there is no other, he falls again and again, into my power."

Having attained everything, these simple-minded people do not understand what lies beyond, deluded as they are by the glamour of worldly possessions. They think they are wise, thinking that this world alone exists and nothing else.

Yama says, "They fall again and again into my power," meaning they fall into the control of Death.

Yama then points out a very important thing: When one begins to understand the Upanishadic dialogue, the Upanishadic teaching, when he says "That" or "He", he is referring to the Supreme Truth or the Supreme Being. And the finding of the Truth, according to the Upanishad, is not a mass phenomenon, but an individual concern. Yama points out:

SHLOKA 7

shravannaaya api bahubhir yo na labhyah
srunvanto api bahavo yam na vidyuh
aashcharyo vaktaa kushala asya labdhaa
aashcharyo jnyaataa kushala anushishtah

"He, who cannot even be heard of, by many; whom many, even though they hear, do not understand; wondrous is he, who can teach and skilful is he who finds Him. Wondrous is he who knows Him, when instructed by the wise."

So, the finding of the Truth, according to the Upanishad, is not a mass phenomenon. It is an individual effort. There is no magic formula which the teacher can give to hundreds of people: "You practice this and you'll reach the Truth." Impossible! As far as the Upanishad, or Shruthi, is concerned, it does not work that way.

The Shruthi says here about the Supreme Being, that many have not heard of Him; many, even though they hear about Him, do not understand. So it is wonderful, if someone can teach It, and it is also more wonderful, if someone is skilful enough to understand what is being taught. Wondrous is he who knows Him, being instructed by the wise. The Supreme Being cannot be understood en mass – it is too subtle.

Why is it so difficult to understand? The basic reason is because the mind is attracted, caught and trapped by the outside world of the senses. Once the mind is free, there is no difficulty in understanding.

But, it is not a joke to free the mind. Look carefully, critically, within your minds, without fooling yourself: You will find that, in the beginning, many *sadhaks* start on earnest *sadhana*. One wants to very seriously discover the Truth and so on. Somewhere along the line, there are temptations, which are not good, naturally. Now, there are some *sadhaks* who say, "Ah! These are temptations. I should overcome them." There are many who get into a new teaching, suddenly, and say, "These temptations are inevitable, so let me carry on!" They are lost!

Then the Upanishad points out that it is not easy for everybody to teach about the Supreme Being. Why is it so? According to the Upanishad, this can be taught only by one who has understood It. If he has not understood and experienced It, It cannot be conveyed. It cannot be taught by word of mouth. That is why it says: "Skilful is he who understands even when the wise teach him," because his mind has to be ready to grasp It; otherwise, the words may go to waste.

Yama continues about the importance of the right teacher who has understood the Supreme Being. He says:

SHLOKA 8

na narenna avarena proktaa esha
suvignyeyo bahudhaa chintyamaanah
ananya prokte gatir atra na asti
anneeyaan hy atarkyam anu pramaannaat

"Taught by an inferior person, He cannot be truly understood, as He is thought of in many ways. Unless It is taught by one who knows

Him, there is no way to understand It. It is inconceivable and subtler than the subtlest."

Yama states that the Supreme Being cannot be taught by an inferior teacher. He, or It, cannot be truly understood because He is thought of in many ways. There are many ways of looking at this Supreme Being. It is infinite – therefore, there are infinite ways of looking at It. So, if a person who has not understood It in Its entirety, teaches, then It cannot be truly understood.

It is inconceivable and subtler than the subtlest. Therefore, unless it is taught by one who knows himself as that Supreme Being; unless the person, who is teaching, has understood that in his inner Self, he is either connected with that Supreme Being or identified with that Supreme Being; unless and until such a person teaches, there is no way to understand It, because It is inconceivable and subtler than the subtlest – *anu pramaanat.*

It is so subtle that It cannot be understood until the student is ready, without any kind of prejudice, to understand It and his mind is looking one-pointedly, only for It. And, It also cannot be understood if the person who teaches has no experience of what he is saying. If both these conditions do not apply, then It cannot be understood.

Then, how do we understand? The way of understanding is called "negation". You slowly take out all that is unnecessary or all that is not applicable; eliminate everything and then what is left is that Supreme Being. This is the Upanishadic teaching. Shankaracharya has said that It is the unreachable substratum, after the negation of all tangible objects.

That means, It is That where the mind cannot reach. Then, how do we see It? Only when the mind has totally settled down, can It be understood. Yama then says:

SHLOKA 9

naishaa tarkena matir aapaneyaa
prokta anyenaiva sujnaanaaya preshtha

yaam tvam aapah satyadhritir bataasi
tvaadrun no bhooyaan nachiketah prashtaa

"Not by reasoning can It be attained, O dearest, but when it is taught by another, who has understood It, It is well understood. You have truly resolved to understand by holding fast to truth. May we get other enquirers like you, O Nachiketas."

Yama is saying, "I wish there was another enquirer as serious and sincere as you in the attempt to understand the Truth. I pray that there are more Nachiketas born, who can understand this Truth. This is not attainable through reason but It is attainable only when It is taught by one who has understood It."

Yama continues saying how difficult it is to reach It. He says:

SHLOKA 10

jaanaamy aham shevadhir ity anityam
na hy adhruvaih praapyate hi dhruvam tat
tato mayaa nachiketas chitah agnir
anityair dravyaih praaptavaan asmi nityam

"I know that wealth is impermanent, not reached through transient things. Yet, by me is laid the Nachiketas-fire, and by impermanent means have I reached the Ever-lasting."

This is a very interesting statement. The previous *shloka* said It cannot be reached either by reason, or by any impermanent means.

The Nachiketas-fire, being in oneself, is after all part of the impermanent world. So, what Yama says is that there is a way of reaching the Permanent through the impermanent world; not through reasoning and dispute and discourse, but when someone who knows It, teaches, then it directly opens the heart, lights the fire. When that fire is lit, it is the connection between the impermanent and the Permanent.

Yama continues to praise Nachiketas. He says:

SHLOKA 11

kaamasya aptim jagatah pratishtaam
krator aanantyam abhayasya paaram
stomaa mahat urugaayam pratishthaam drushtvaa
dhrutyaa dheero nachiketo atyasraaksheeh

"Having seen the fulfilment of all desires, the support of the world, the endless fruit of all the rites, the other shore, where there is no fear; having also seen the greatness of fame, the far-stretching, the foundation of everything, you, O Nachiketas, have still held steadfastly to the Truth and firmly rejected everything."

Yama then tells Nachiketas how one can access that Supreme Being. How can It be realised? He says:

SHLOKA 12

tam durdarsham goodham anupravishtham
guhaahitam gahvareshtam puraanam
adhyaatma yogaadhigamena devam
matvaa dheero harsha shokau jahaati

"Realising through Self-contemplation that Primeval God, the Supreme Being, difficult to be seen, deeply hidden in the cave of the heart, dwelling subtly within; when the wise man reaches That in meditation, he leaves behind both joy as well as sorrow."

Yama says that the Supreme Being can be realised through Self-contemplation – not by looking for It in words, or in discourses. When It is looked for within, the wise man, through meditation, realises the Supreme Being dwelling subtly within the deep cave of his heart. When he reaches That, he leaves behind both joy and sorrow.

Normally, if there is some joy, there is always some sorrow following it, and if there is sorrow, we always live with the hope that around the corner, there might be some joy still to come. But, in this state, where one leaves behind both joy and sorrow, there is the ultimate *shanti.* And that, says Yama, is realised through Self-contemplation on that Primeval God.

You need not search for It anywhere outside – look for It in the cave of your own heart and see it in the secret recesses of your heart. No more do joy and sorrow exist, which means, no more are pleasure and pain there. One is beyond pleasure and pain.

It may be a little difficult, in the beginning, to theoretically understand the Upanishadic statements about the Supreme Being. For instance, as the Kena Upanishad declares, *na tatra chakshur gacchatti na vaag gacchatti no manah*: "Where the eye does not go, nor does the ear, nor does the mind." This is incomprehensible! If the eye does not go there, okay, I can still hear about It. But, if the ear too does not go there, then what do I do? Okay, I have my mind. But, if even the mind does not reach there, then how do I find It? So it becomes an inscrutable mystery.

But, in the Upanishad itself, you discover what it actually means. As long as I am trying to find It, there is still the element of "I" in it and I cannot find It. So, what the Upanishad says is when the mind is totally quiet and calm, not reaching out anywhere, whether into this world or into the other; when it has completely settled down, is silent, then that Truth is revealed. So, although the Upanishadic statements appear to be contradictory and paradoxical sometimes, if you look at them seriously and carefully, you will find that there is some sense in them.

Also, the Upanishadic teachings are somewhat like Zen teachings; trying to prove that there are certain things that cannot be attained by way of linear logic: "I am here, I have to go there; therefore, I have to travel this distance." But the Supreme Being is here, there and everywhere simultaneously. In trying to study about the Supreme Being, the Ishavasya Upanishad declares *isha vaasyam idam sarvam*: "That Supreme Being pervades everything here" – there is no question of going from one point to another.

Therefore, in some places, the Upanishad uses the language of paradox and contradiction to break down our usual shells of logical thinking. In this context, sometimes two plus two equals five. But then, this is somewhat like the difference between Newtonian physics and Quantum physics. In Quantum physics, everything is uncertain. It is called the Uncertainty Principle. In Newtonian physics, everything is certain and this is applicable to our day-to-day life. But, when we go to the higher plane things become uncertain. Thus, the difference between the Upanishadic teaching and other kind of teaching can be equated to the difference between Quantum physics and Newtonian physics.

Here, we are dealing with the imponderables and yet one has to touch It, otherwise there is no point in going through the whole exercise. The Upanishad does not say, "Abandon It because you cannot find It." Instead it says, "Look carefully and you will find It, but not the way you usually think you can find It." That's why, sometimes, it gets a little confusing.

The Upanishadic teachings are those which have to be listened to, thought over, understood and realised and made one's own experience. That is why the student must go through *shravanam mananam nidhidyasa* – you first listen; then think about what you have listened to and carefully put your mind to it. When what the teacher has been trying to teach has been understood, then it is made one's own experience.

SHLOKA 13

etat shrutvaa samparigrihya martyah
pravruhya dharmyam anum etam aapya
sa modate modaneeyam hi labdhvaa
vivrutam sadma nachiketasam manye

"Hearing about this and comprehending It, a mortal extracts the essence of the subtle and rejoices, having reached the source of all joy. Such an abode of peace, which is understood by comprehending this Truth, is wide open unto Nachiketas."

Nachiketas then asks Yama this question:

SHLOKA 14

anyatra dharmaat anyatra adharmaat
anyatra asmaat krutakrutaat
anyatra bhootaats cha bhavyaats cha
yat tat pashyasi tat vada

"Tell me that which you see beyond right and wrong; beyond what is done or not done; beyond the past and the future. Please tell me."

If a thing has a past and future, it definitely belongs to this world because the moment we look at the present, it has shifted to the past. Even a thought: the moment you have thought, it has been thought already, and gone. When we study something and get what we call knowledge, it goes into memory and it is past. And when we want to recall it, then we have to go back, recollect and retrieve it. So, none of these things can be the everlasting Reality, because the everlasting Reality should not disappear with the future and become the past. It has to be present always, as It is.

Nachiketas asks, "Do you know of something, O Yama; which is beyond right and wrong?" That means, a state where once one reaches, the ordinary concepts of right and wrong do not remain. Please understand that the Upanishad is not advocating that you should be a Bohemian and have no discretion between right and wrong. As the Upanishad proceeds, you will see that the only approach to It, is through goodness and righteousness.

Yama says, "Now I will let you in, a little more, into this state." He says:

SHLOKA 15

sarve vedaa yat padam aamananti
tapaamsi sarvaani cha yad vadanti
yad icchanto brahmacharayam charanti
tat te padam sangrahenna braveemi aum ity etat

"That Word, which all the Vedas declare, desiring which, people perform austerities to attain and live the life of a religious student, *brahmacharya;* that Word, I will declare to you in brief. It is *Aum.*"

The entire Vedas and the Upanishads declare *om* or *aum* as the One Word, the One Truth. People perform austerities and live the life of a religious student, or *brahmacharya,* to attain That Supreme Being, the Brahman, who is none other than that word *Aum.* "That *charya,* or that activity, which takes you to the Brahman," this is the meaning of *brahmacharya.*

In the Mandukya Upanishad, *om* or *aum,* is described as the symbol of the different states of consciousness: "*a*" is for the waking state or *jaagrit;* "*u*" is for the dream state or *svapna;* and "*m*" or "*im*" is for the deep sleep state or *sushupti.* And beyond the three is what is known as the *turiya,* which is the Witness of all the three states.

When one understands that Witness, one knows that all these states are relatively unreal when compared to each other. For instance, in a dream, you are chased by a tiger – you run fast, the tiger is after you; it has almost caught you.You wake up; there is no tiger, but you are still sweating, your heart is pounding. It is very real. In the dream, if somebody said it was unreal, you wouldn't believe it but when you wake up, it is actually unreal. So in the dream state, the waking state is unreal and in the waking state, the dream state is a dream. Now, these states are relative to each other; real only when they exist, unreal, when they don't.

But there is a Witness who witnesses and is conscious and aware of all that is happening, and that is known as the *turiya.* And all this is represented by *aum*: *a, u, im,* represent the three states of consciousness, which are normally known to us and the *ardha matra* of *aum* is the last ringing sound, which comes after you chant *aum,* the *mmm* sound, which goes on in the end, like the ringing of the bell – that is the *turiya.* This, in brief, is the *aum.*

Let us now come to the philosophical part of it. Those who are in the practice of *sadhana,* will know that in the deep stages of meditation, one begins to hear the sound of the *pranava aum,* within, and that is the link to moving into the higher realms of consciousness. Some schools of philosophy or religious teachings call it the *surat shabdha,* by which one proceeds further up. It is known as the *pranava dhvani* and also the *anaahata shabdha.*

Describing the syllable *aum* further, Yama says:

SHLOKA 16

etadd hy evaakshram brahma etadd hy evaakshram param
etadd hy evaakshram jnaatvaa yo yad icchati tasya tat

"This syllable *aum* is verily the everlasting Brahman; this syllable indeed is the highest end; knowing this very syllable, whatever one desires, that indeed will be his."

It means, if you understand what that *aum* is, you have understood the entire mystery of the universe and have attained everything. It does not mean that if I keep chanting *aum* and I desire a new tape-recorder, it will fall into my lap! That is not the meaning of the Upanishad. The Upanishad does not discuss such matters.

It means, when you have understood the meaning of that syllable *aum,* you have attained everything that is to be attained. The aim of life, therefore, is to understand that *aum.*

Continuing about the significance of *aum,* Yama says:

SHLOKA 17

etad aalambanam sreshtham etad aalambanam param
etad aalambanam jnaatvaa brahmaloke maheeyate

"This support is the best; this support is the supreme. Knowing this support, one is worshipped in Brahmaloka, the World of Brahma."

Yama then says, "I must tell you the qualities of that inner Self, your true identity, by understanding which, you are free of joy and sorrow and are not disturbed by any of the opposites." He says:

SHLOKA 18

na jaayate mriyate va vipashchit
na aayam kutashchinn na babhuva kashchit
ajo nityah shashvoto yam purano
na hanyate hanyamaane sharirey

"That Self, which is the knowing Self, is never born nor does It ever die. It has sprung from nothing and nothing springs from It. It is unborn, eternal, abiding and primeval. It is not slain when the body is slain."

This is also expressed in the Bhagavad Gita, a little differently. It means, that Self, which is the Witness, the knower – not that which is known – is like the eye that sees everything. But the eye does not see itself – we see the eye's reflection in the mirror. But, because the eye does not see itself, we cannot say it does not exist. It is because of the existence of the eye that the whole world is seen. This Brahman, or the Supreme Self, is like the eye – It is the Seer of everything and although it is not seen by itself, it knows that it exists because it sees everything else.

Harinama Sankirtana, which is chanted in the evenings in many homes in Kerala, is supposed to be a *bhakti* song, but it is quite philosophical. It means: "The 'eye' of the eye is the 'eye' of the mind; when I realise that I am the 'eye' of the mind, how joyous it is."

The Self, the eternal Self, which is your true identity, is never born nor does It die. If one gets really fixed on this firm foundation of understanding of one's own inner Self, one is no more identified with the body, but is identified with the Self. What fear or unhappiness is there for such a person? When I say, "I am that Self which is never born" – not merely say but understand and realize – "I remain always the same. When the body is slain, I am not slain."

Yama continues:

SHLOKA 19

hantaa chen manyate hantum hatah chen manyate hatam
ubhau tau na vijaaneeto naayam hanti na hanyate

"If the slayer who kills thinks that he slays, or if the slain thinks that he is being slain, both of them do not understand It. It neither slays nor is It slain."

The slayer and the slain do not understand It because it is the body which is being slain; the Self cannot be slain. The Upanishad is not saying, "You go and slay somebody." Once you read and understand something, you have to look at the other aspect, because there are people who look only at one side. We cannot help that.

So the real Self is not slain, nor does one who thinks he slays It, slay It. It is always existent, without any change.

Yama continues with the description of the Self:

SHLOKA 20

anor aneeyaan mahato maheeyaan
aatmaasya jantor nihito guhaayaam
tam akratuh pashyati veetashoko
dhaatuprasaadaan mahimaanam aatmanah

"It is smaller than the small and greater than the great; yet, the Self is seated in the hearts of every creature. The unstriving man, free from sorrow, through tranquility of the mind and the senses, sees the greatness of the Self."

The Upanishad is trying to lead you into something which is difficult to grasp by the so-called rational mind, which knows that one plus one equals two. When we go to deeper aspects, there is a certain element of uncertainty, which means that it can be understood only when one goes beyond the ordinary, practical, rational mind. But, rationality is very important, please understand. It is only the rational mind which can understand that it has its limitations. This is the teaching of the Upanishad – not that you have to ban it, but to realise its limitations. This is also the prayer of the Gayatri Mantra – "Illumine my intelligence so that I may understand its limitations." The intellect is useful in its own place, there is no doubt, but beyond a certain point, it cannot move; and we are looking for the Source from which intelligence originates, the core of consciousness.

Therefore, the only way this can be described is: "It is smaller than the small" or "bigger than the big" and so on, because you cannot really say what It is. Even air cannot be described, leave alone the Brahman! This description of being "smaller than the small, greater than the great" is a contradiction in the ordinary world because if something is "smaller than the small" it cannot at the same time be "greater than the great." So, it means that it is trying, through contradictions, to prove the existence of something that is beyond conception. "It is smaller than the small and greater than the great; the Self is seated in the heart of every creature", also means It is all-pervading and yet It can be contacted in the heart of every creature – fortunately!

"The unstriving man beholds Him, freed from sorrow": What is the meaning of "unstriving"? *akratuh* is the word used – it means "one who does not strive." This can mean two things: "the unstriving man" can be one who has understood the futility of striving for pleasures in this world. It can also mean that while in meditation, one strives in the beginning to reach a certain point; after that, one lets go and remains quiet and settled.

The Zen Buddhists have described it beautifully by saying how an arrow and a bow are used to shoot a target. You need a bow, you need an arrow, you need a human mind, you need the eye, and you need intelligence. Then, you need energy to pull the arrow and the bowstring and you need the target. You keep the target and the arrow to your eye, in the same line. You pull the bowstring taut – now everything is ready. Then, if you have to hit the target, what will you do? Will you let go the arrow, or will you hold on? Can one deny that the exercise of holding it straight is necessary? But, after a point, is it necessary? It is not. You have to throw the bow and the arrow.

So, *akratuh* is one who does not strive. He understands the futility of striving and he lets go. In such a case, the mind is tranquil, the senses are tranquil. Remaining quiet and settled, he beholds that Supreme Being, freed from sorrow. That is also the meaning of surrender. But that surrender will not come to an intellectual, until he is intellectually convinced that he has to surrender. The simple man may surrender straight away and throw the bow and arrow and say, "Take me."

But that is not possible for the thinking human being, who has to think and find out that one should surrender. That's fine – that is how intelligent people go about it. But ultimately, one has to transcend the intellect. There is a wrong concept among some people that one can attain the Supreme Being intellectually. This is not possible.

It is only when we understand, through subtle and higher intelligence, that it is impossible for the limited brain to reach that Supreme Being, that it may be possible to reach it. This is the teaching of the Upanishad.

So the unstriving man, free from sorrow, through tranquility of the mind and senses beholds the greatness of the Self.

Yama continues giving contradictory descriptions of the Supreme Being. He says:

SHLOKA 21

aaseeno dooram vrajati shayaano yaati sarvatah
kastam madaamadam devam mad anyo jnaatum arhati

"Sitting, He moves far; lying down, He goes everywhere."

"Who, save me, can know that God, who rejoices and rejoices not?"

"Sitting, He moves far; lying down, He goes everywhere": this description of the Supreme Being means that It is all-pervading. It is not, and cannot be, confined to a single place. If It is sitting here, It is also there. Even in my own small way, I may be sitting here, but my mind can be elsewhere. It is possible. How is it possible for me to sit here and also be away from here? Because my mind has come from That which is all-pervading. This is not possible for a human being, except in a dream. It is not impossible for the Supreme Being.

Yama then says:

SHLOKA 22

ashareeram shareereshu anavastheshu avasthitam
mahaantam vibhum aatmaanam matvaa dheero na shochati

"Knowing the Self, who is bodiless among the bodies; the stable among the unstable; the great and the all-pervading, the wise man does not grieve."

Knowing that Supreme Self, who is hidden in the heart, but is also all-pervading, who is the most stable among unstable things, who is bodiless although present in all bodies – knowing that Self, the wise man does not grieve.

Here comes a real shock. Yama says:

SHLOKA 23

naayam aatmaa pravachane na labhyo
na medhayaa na bahunaa shrutena
yamevaisha vrineete tena labhyas
tasyaisha aatmaa vivrineete tanoom svaam

"This Self cannot be attained by instruction, or by intellectual power, or even through much hearing. He is to be attained only by the one whom He chooses. To such a one, the Self reveals His own nature."

This does not mean that it is futile to try to understand the Supreme Self. The meaning of this statement, which is connected to what was said before, is that this Supreme Self cannot be attained by following what one was instructed to do, because there is no step by step instruction like, "If you stand on your head for fifteen hours, you will see the Supreme Brahman," or, "If you read a particular book, you will see the Supreme Brahman." One may do all this; yet if the mind has not become stable and quiet, the experience is impossible. Mere instruction is of little help – the person should also be ready for instruction. Mere intellectual power is not enough. If that was the case, all the great intellectuals would be God-realised, which is not always true, because, one may listen to many lectures, but still one has not found the Truth. So, It is not attained through much hearing.

Then, how is It attained? It is attained by the one whom the Self chooses. "To such a one, the Self reveals his own nature." When will the Self choose one? When you realize that you are helpless, the Self chooses you.

To illustrate this point, once while sitting in a cave and shivering in the cold, my Master gave me this interesting example: Imagine that there is an open glass box, with a division in-between, which is also made of glass. On one side there is a beautiful section with a lot of greenery and garden; and the other side is dry and drab with not even water.

There are these little, wafer-thin creatures on either side. There are very few, just one or two creatures, blue in colour, on the beautiful garden side, while the dry side is full of red creatures, in plenty. But there is one peculiarity in these wafer-thin red creatures, which is that they know only two-dimensions – length and breadth. They do not know of the third dimension, height or depth. It is possible for them to move only in the direction they know, that is either along the length or the breadth.

Through this dividing wall of glass, the red ones see those other guys, the blue ones, enjoying themselves in the beautiful greenery. They too want to go there but since they know only two dimensions, they keep moving sideways, trying to go the other side. They try and try. But they do not have any concept of the dimension called "up". Even though the top of the box is open, they are powerless to go up. They only know length and breadth and so they keep moving sideways.

Standing out of it, you can look into the box and see the antics of these beings, going round and round. You wonder why they don't climb across and go over to the other side, and then you realise that these fellows do not have the capacity, they do not know that dimension. You very much want to catch them and put them on the other side, but, how can you choose them when they are all the time moving and trying, on their own? You try to catch them, but they keep moving, desperately trying to get out.

One of these creatures, after having tried everything, goes to a corner and says, "I think this is not possible. There is no way – let me be still." So when he stops moving, you pick him up and put him on the other side. "Ah! Here I am!" he exclaims. Such stories have their imperfections but they illustrate a point.

Therefore, the Supreme Self chooses one, when one has completely understood that the only way is to settle down and become quiet. "To such a one, the Self reveals His own nature."

Since this has been declared, it may be misinterpreted. We can say that we can do whatever we like but ultimately, the Self will choose us! Many people use this as an excuse and if you are satisfied with this world, it's fine. But it is not an excuse for a *sadhaka*. So, there is a clarification which follows immediately after.

What is the clarification? Yama says:

SHLOKA 24

na avirato dushcharitaan naashanto naasamaahitah
naashanta maanaso vaapi prajnaanenainam aapnuyaat

"Not he, who has not desisted from evil ways; not he, who is not tranquil; not he, who has not a concentrated mind; not he whose mind is not composed, can reach this Self, even through right knowledge."

So, none can reach that Self "even through right knowledge, until the Self chooses to reveal Itself." However, this is not an excuse and *sadhana* has to be practised. What the Upanishad says is that this Self cannot be reached by somebody who has not desisted from evil ways, who has not tried and achieved the technique of becoming tranquil, who has not a concentrated mind, whose mind is not composed. These are all part of *sadhana* and have to be practiced to have the qualification to know the Self.

Yama continues:

SHLOKA 25

yasya brahma cha kshatram cha ubhe bhavata odanah
mrityur yasyopasechanam ka itthaa veda yatra sah

"That Supreme Being, for whom priesthood and nobility are as food, and Death as a sauce – who really knows where He is?"

That Supreme Being, "for whom the Brahmin and the Kshatriya are like food" – that means He eats them up in no time. "For whom even Death is like a sauce"- He adds that in and eats them up. Who really knows where that Supreme Being is? How is it possible to know that Supreme Being? What is the way to know that Supreme Being? For that, one has to understand the limitations of one's capacity to reach It and therefore to let go and relax, and then what takes place is called surrender. It comes to various people at various times – there is a pace for everybody. For some, it comes early; for some, it comes late and there are multifarious reasons for that.

CHAPTER 3

Yama continues his teaching. He says:

SHLOKA 1

hritam pibantau sukritasya loke
guhaam pravishtau parame paraardhe
chaayaa tapau brahmavido vadanti
panchaagnayo ye cha tri naachiketaah

"There are two Selves that drink the fruit of *karma* in the world of good deeds. Both are lodged in the secret place of the heart, which is the seat of the Supreme Being. The knowers of Brahman as well as those householders who maintain the five sacrificial-fires and perform the Nachiketa-rite speak of these two Selves as light and shade."

The Upanishad clarifies that "the knowers of Brahman" or "the knowers of the Truth" are not only the *sannyasins* who have given up the world; they are also "those householders who maintain the five sacrificial fires and perform the Nachiketa-rite." It includes all human beings, irrespective of whether they are renunciants or living in the world.

They, who have known that Supreme Being, speak of these two Selves who reside in the heart, as "light and shade" or "light and shadow". That means, one is "real" and the other is the "shadow". The "real" is the one who enjoys, without being involved. And the "shade" or the "shadow" is that self which actually thinks it is rejoicing and therefore, it is also suffering when it is not rejoicing. Or, when the joy or the source of joy is taken away, it suffers. When we have no joy, that itself is suffering. Of these, that which is known as the "shadow" is the unreal self, which is our mind. Therefore, to realise that one's true identity is not that "shadow" called the mind, but that which is Conscious and is yet not affected by any of these – that, is the teaching of the Upanishad.

Yama says:

SHLOKA 2

yah setur eejaanaanaam aksharam brahma yat param
abhayam titeershatam paaram naachiketam shakemahi

"Those who wish to be free and cross over to the other side, perform the Nachiketa-fire sacrifice. May we master that fire sacrifice, which is the bridge to the fearless shore, which is the highest, imperishable Brahman!"

This is a prayer seeking to master that technique known as the Nachiketa-fire sacrifice, the bridge by which one crosses to the other shore of absolute fearlessness.

Yama compares the body to a chariot and the Self is the Lord within. He says:

SHLOKA 3

aatmaanam rathinam viddhi shareeram ratham eva tu
buddhim tu saarathim viddhi manah pragraham eva cha

"Know the Supreme Self as the Lord of the chariot and the body as the chariot. Know the intellect as the charioteer and the mind as the reins."

Yama continues:

SHLOKA 4

indriyaani hayaan aahur vishayaams teshu gocharaan
atma indriya mano yuktam bhokta iti aahur manishinah

"The senses are the horses, the objects of the senses are the paths through which they travel. The wise declare the Self, associating with the body, the senses and the mind as the enjoyer."

Yama describes that the Self, the *atman,* is the Lord of the chariot. The body, the intellect is the charioteer. The mind is the rein. The senses are the horses. The objects of the senses are the paths which they take and the Self, associating with all this, enjoys the whole thing, the whole activity.

Yama tells Nachiketas about the mind and its role in reaching our goal. He says:

SHLOKA 5

yas tu avijnyaanavaan bhavaty ayuktena manasaa sadaa
tasya indriyaani avashyaani dushtaashvaa iva saaratheh

"Therefore, he who has no understanding, whose mind is always unrestrained, his senses are out of control, just as wicked horses are for a charioteer."

How can such a person reach his goal, whose horses are wanton and do not obey his command?

SHLOKA 6

yas tu vijnaanavaan bhavati yuktena manasaa sadaa
tasya indriyaani vashyaani sadashvaa iva saaratheh

"However, he who has understanding, whose mind is always restrained, has his senses under control – they are like good horses to a charioteer."

Yama continues telling Nachiketas about one who has no understanding, who has no control over his mind. Such a person does not attain his goal, but comes back into mundane life. He says:

SHLOKA 7

yas tu avijnyaanavaan bhavaty amanaskas sadaa shuchih
na sa tat padam aapnoti samsaaram cha adhigacchati

"One who has no understanding and has no control over his wandering mind, and is impure, reaches not that goal but comes back again and again into mundane life."

Practically, another way of looking at this is, when one thinks of this world, it means that instead of remaining, or being able to remain at rest in the inner Being, one returns repeatedly into the turbulent world.

Yama continues:

SHLOKA 8

yas tu vijnaanavaan bhavati samanaskas sadaa shuchih
sa tu tat padam aapnoti yasmaad bhooyo na jaayate

"However, he who has understanding, who has control over his mind, and is pure, reaches that goal from which he is not born again."

Again, we can interpret it for here and for the hereafter: either the soul does not come back because it is free, or the one whose mind is pure and has understanding is free from the sorrows of this world. He who is calm, quiet, restrained and pure, is "not born again", meaning, nothing more that can cause sorrow for him is born in his mind. Normally, whenever we get some peace, something comes up and again we are caught up in the world. So what the Upanishad is saying is that in that state, there is no more getting caught in this circle – you are free!

That does not mean that the realised man does not have problems like all of us do, but his way of looking at the problems, facing them and dealing with them is different from what is normally done.

We all know that Ramana Maharishi had cancer. Many other people also have cancer but there is a difference between the Maharishi and them. The Maharishi lived with the understanding that he was not the body. So even if he had some pain at some point, that pain did not affect his inner Self, of which he was very aware. Whereas an ordinary person, who is identified with the body, would think that is the end and there is a great deal of suffering also because he has to leave all that he considers to be the dearest and the nearest to himself. The one who is realised, like the Maharishi, sees that the inner Self is the dearest and the nearest.

Yama says that the goal can be reached by a man of self-control. He says:

SHLOKA 9

vijnaana saarathir yastu manah pragrahavaan narah
sa adhvanah param aapnoti tad vishnoh paramam padam

"He, who drives with this understanding, becomes the clever driver of his chariot and controls the reins of his mind. He surely reaches the end of his journey, which is the Supreme Abode of Vishnu."

"Vishnu" means "the all-pervading Self" – present everywhere. So the man of discrimination and self control attains the supreme goal of life, the abode of Vishnu.

Then Yama gives a step by step description about the connection between this world and That. He says:

SHLOKA 10

indriyebhyah paraa hy arthaa arthebhyas cha param manah
manasas cha paraa buddhir buddher aatmaa mahaan parah

"Beyond the senses are the objects, beyond the objects is the mind, beyond the mind is the intelligence and beyond the intelligence or the understanding is the Great Self, the *mahaan atman.*"

The sense objects are beyond the senses because the senses are meaningless if there are no objects. In deep sleep, the senses are there but they are of no use because there are no objects for the senses.

"Beyond the objects is the mind": That which attaches the senses to the objects is *manah*- the mind or thought. The whole bundle of thoughts that we have is called the mind.

"Beyond the mind is *buddhi"* – the intelligence or what can be called the understanding. What is this understanding? It is that which is seeing the mind and also understanding: "Ah! This is my mind. It is functioning, it is thinking. I should think, I should not think." That is what is known here as "the understanding" which is beyond the mind.

"Beyond the understanding is the *mahaan atman*" – the Great Self, which is the core of one's consciousness, which is within, which is the Witness.

That is not all, as Yama continues grading what is existent in the scale of what is the subtlest. He says:

SHLOKA 11

mahatah param avyaktam
avyaktaat purushah parah
purushaan na param kinchit:
sa kaashtaa saa paraa gatih

"Beyond that Great Self is the Unmanifest – *avyaktam* – and beyond the Unmanifest is the Spirit – the *purusha*. That *purusha* is the final goal – that is the end of the journey. There is nothing beyond."

Beyond that Great Self, which is the Witness, which watches everything – all the activities of the senses, the mind and the intellect – is the Unmanifest, the *avyaktam,* which is the Mind, considered not as the mind of an individual, but as the sum total of all minds, the universal Mind.

Actually, if you look at it, there is one universal Mind that manifests through different centres or different brains. Try to figure it out: you have some sorrow, I have some sorrow and a third person also has some sorrow. Your sorrow and the cause of your sorrow may be different from my sorrow and the cause of my sorrow. It may be different, but the fact remains that we all have sorrow – it is a common factor.

So also is joy. Your joy may be different. For you, joy may be having a nice puff after a long time and my joy may be having idli and chutney powder. But, the joy is a common factor.

In the same way, there is one sorrow in the whole world and it manifests itself for different reasons through different people at different times. That is the *avyakta* – Mind.

"Beyond the *avyaktam* is the *purusha*"- the Spirit. The word *purusha* shows it is not "nothingness" or an impersonal object. Here, *purusha* means a conscious entity, but not a limited entity. And that *purusha* is the final goal, the end of the journey. There is nothing beyond That.

The Buddhists also believe, "That is the end, beyond which there is no movement; it is the other shore" – *tad yatha gatha gathe para gathe para samgathe bodhi svaha.*

Many of these terms, although they are in the Upanishads, can be found in the Samkhya philosophy, like the word *purusha.* The first mention of *purusha* is in the Rig Veda, in the Purusha Suktam – *sahasrashirshapurushah sahasraaksha sahasrapaad.*

Later, when Kapila Muni introduced his system of philosophy known as the Samkhya Yoga, he incorporated many terms from the Upanishads. In fact, *yoga* is one part of Samkhya philosophy. And Kapila Muni is very important, because, in the Bhagavad Gita, when

Krishna lists his *mahimas,* he says, "Among the mountains, I am Meru; among the Vedas, I am Sama Veda; among the *munis,* I am Kapila."

So the great *muni,* Kapila, brought out the Samkhya system of philosophy, which is an excellent system of cosmology too. It begins with *purusha prakriti* and how the world comes into being and so on. In fact, there is a beautiful description of *prakriti* in the Samkhya Pravachana Sutra. It says, *prakaroti iti prakriti* – "that which divides and creates division is *prakriti.*"And unity is that which goes back to the *purusha.* So that is the final goal, that *purusha,* who is beyond even the totality of thinking and the Mind.

Yama continues about the hidden Spirit, *purusha.* He says:

SHLOKA 12

esha sarveshu bhooteshu gooddho aatma na prakaashate
drushyate tvagryayaa buddhyaa sookshmayaa sookshma darshibhih

"That Self, *atman,* though hidden in all beings, does not shine forth visibly. It can only be seen by the seers through the sharp and subtle understanding or intelligence."

That Self, that *purusha,* is "hidden in all beings". It is not as if It belongs only to the teacher of the Upanishad, but It is hidden in all beings. Therefore, in that way, everybody is equal, as the Self is hidden in all beings. That is the kind of equality which is the best – it has no caste, no creed, no race, and no religion.

That *atman* is hidden in all beings and does not shine forth. It is not evident when you look at a being that there is this inner Self, this *purusha* inside. It can be seen by the seers with subtle minds, through their sharp intelligence and subtle understanding. They see the Self within.

Then Yama tells Nachiketas how the wise attain a peaceful state. He says:

SHLOKA 13

yacched vaang manasee praajnyas
tad yacched jnyaana aatmani

jnyaanam aatmani mahati niyacchet
tad yacchet shaanta aatmani

"The wise should merge the speech in the mind and that mind in the intellect; the intellect in the Great Self and that Great Self in the Self of Peace."

After saying all that, the *rishi* of the Upanishad urges not to be complacent. Yama says to Nachiketas:

SHLOKA 14
uttishthata jaagrata praapya varaan nibodhata
kshoorayasya dhaaraa nishitaa duratyayaa
durgam pathas tat kavayo vadanti

"Arise! Awake! Having attained all your boons, understand them. This path that you are taking is like the sharp edge of a razor, difficult and hard to cross – so the great sages have declared."

Swami Vivekananda was very fond of this statement "Arise! Awake!" Some people translate it as "stop not till the goal is reached." But I would say, "Now that you have got your boons, understand them."

Yama urges Nachiketas not to be complacent. He says, "Now that you have attained all your boons, do not be complacent but try to understand them and realise the Self. Be awake, be careful because this path that you are taking is as sharp as the edge of a razor and is hard to cross. The great sages have declared that it is a difficult path to cross."

In ancient Vedic terminology, *kavi* is not just a "poet" but it also means "the wise". "The wise" that have the revelation or understanding of the Truth and therefore sing about it in ecstasy are called *kavi.*

Yama then describes the Self, the *atman,* knowing which, one is free from the fear of death. He says:

SHLOKA 15
ashabdam asparsham aroopam avyayam
tathaa arasam nityam agandhavac cha yat

anaadyanantam mahatah param dhruvam
nichaayya tam mrityu mukhaat pramuchyate

"That Self is without sound, without touch, without form, without decay; It cannot be tasted or smelled; It is eternal and has no beginning or end; It is immutable and beyond the Great Self. Discerning that and abiding in It, one is free from the fear of death."

What Yama is saying is, "Awake! Arise! Understand, Nachiketas, that you are not the little fellow who you think you are, but you are that formless, greater than the greatest, the Self which can be neither destroyed nor is born, that ever-existing Supreme Self. Knowing that Self and abiding in that Peace be free from the fear of death."

That means, if one is That Self then there is no fear of death. Where is death going to take us? It is only when I am identified with my little self, there is fear. So, understand this, apply your mind to it and don't be complacent till you reach the goal.

Now, this is a great message. It is a message of strength and greatness. It is not a message of weakness and littleness. In fact, the Chandogya Upanishad declares, "*naayam atma balahine na labhya*" – "This *atma* cannot be attained by the weak." This does not mean that you have to have biceps to do that – what you need is grit. The Upanishad itself declares and those who have experienced It have also found that within all individuals, there is That Supreme Reality, which is powerful, peaceful, eternal and unending. Even to think about It theoretically, one is filled with a certain greatness.

What happens when we relate this story or hear it? Yama says:

SHLOKA 16

naachikatam upaakhyaanam mrutyuproktam sanaatanam
uktvaa shrutvaa cha medhaavee brahmaloke maheeyate

"By hearing or relating this ancient story of Nachiketas, as told by Death, a wise man grows great in the world of Brahman."

The one who tells this ancient story and the one who hears it, "goes up" in his level of consciousness, because by listening to it, even if it does not register, it will linger somewhere inside. Yama repeats:

SHLOKA 17

ya imam paramam guhyam
shraavayet brahma samsadi
prayatah shraadha kaale vaa
tad aanantyaaya kalpate

"Whoever shall have this supreme, mysterious story recited before an assembly of serious seekers, or devoutly repeated at the time of the ceremonies for the dead, will prepare him for everlasting life. This will prepare him for everlasting life!"

In the Tibetan Book of the Dead and the Egyptian Book of the Dead, it is said that when a person is passing away, he does not know where he is going. He is in anxiety, generally. When it says, "at the time of the ceremonies for the dead," it means the ceremonies while the person is dying, not after he has gone. At that time, if someone chants this to him and he listens to it, he goes with perfect peace and understanding, knowing that he is not this little body or this individual self, and that he is going into eternity.

With this, Part 1 of the Katha Upanishad ends. Some scholars are of the opinion that this is the end of the Katha Upanishad.

The section that follows has been added to the body of the Upanishad, to make clearer what has been discussed.

Part 2: CHAPTER 4

This section is a corollary to all that has been discussed in Part 1; it is like a commentary. The *rishi* of the Upanishad says:

SHLOKA 1

paraanchi khaani vyatrunnat svayambhooh
tasmaat paraang pashyati na antaraatman
kaschid dheerah pratyag aatmaanam aikshad
aavritta chakshur amritatvam icchan

"That Self is not to be found through the senses. That Supreme Self has pierced outwards, the openings of the senses. Therefore, one looks outward and not within oneself. Only the wise man, seeking life eternal, with his eyes turned inward, beholds the inner *atman,* the Immortal Self."

The senses cannot find that Self. Just as the eye sees everything but cannot see itself because it is the sense of sight, in the same way, that Supreme Being, the Self, activates the senses and therefore, the senses cannot see It. It is from this Self that the senses proceed outwardly. Therefore, one does not normally look within oneself. Only a wise man, not satisfied with all this impermanence, turns within and sees the Immortal Self. When most look outwards, he looks within and beholds the immortal Self.

SHLOKA 2

paraachah kaamaan anuyanti baalah
te mrityor yanti vitatasya paasham
atha dheera amritatvam viditvaa
dhruvam adruveshu iha na praarthayante

"The small-minded go after outward pleasure and they walk into the snare of the wide-spread death. The wise, however, recognising life eternal, do not try to find the stable among the unstable things of this world."

Death has laid a snare in this world of the senses. The ignorant go after pleasure, rather than the good and they walk into the snare. But the wise do not fall into this snare – they know that they cannot find stability in this unstable world. Then:

SHLOKA 3

yena roopam rasam gandham shabdaan sparshaams
cha maithunaan
etenaiva vijaanaati kim atra parishishyate
etad vai tat

"That, because of which one perceives form, tastes, smells, hears sounds and feels the touches of love; by That alone one perceives that Self. So what is there in this world that remains unknown to That Supreme Self? This verily is That Self. "

It is because of the presence of that inner Self that one experiences this world. There is nothing that is unknown to that Self, which experiences everything, although we think that we are experiencing. After going within and finding out that true Self, hidden in the recesses of the heart, the *rishi* discovers that, what is hidden here, is also what is outside; that which is inside is also there. That which is here is also there.

SHLOKA 4

svapnaan tam jaagaritaantam cha ubhau yena anupashyati
mahaantam vibhum aatmaanam matvaa dheero na shochati

"Having known That Great Omnipresent Self, by which one perceives the waking and dream states, the wise man grieves no more."

There is a Witness which perceives the waking state, which perceives the dream state, which apparently, is also present when one is in deep sleep, without dreams, because when we wake up, we are left with the feeling, "Ah! That was wonderful!" So there is a Witness, but we are not aware of it. And that is the Omnipresent Self, "omnipresent" because It is present in all states of consciousness. That Self perceives all these states. Having known That Omnipresent Self, no more does sorrow touch the wise man who has realised the Supreme Being.

SHLOKA 5

ya imam madhvadam veda aatmaanam jeevam antikaat
eeshaanam bhoota-bhavyasya na tato vijugupsate
etad vai tat

"He who knows this Self, the experiencer, the Lord of both past and present, the living Spirit, close at hand, he knows no fear thereafter. This is verily That."

There is another statement that expresses this, "He is nearer to you than your own jugular vein."

So this Self, the experiencer is verily That Brahman. This is verily That.

SHLOKA 6

yaa poorvam tapaso jaatam adbhyah poorvam ajaayata
guhaam pravishya tishthantam yo bhootebhir yapashyata
etad vai tat

"He was born of old from austerity. He was born before the waters. That Being, who is from the beginning, having entered the secret place of the heart and dwelling with the elements, looks forth through the beings. This is verily That."

"He was born of old through austerity": this refers to the story in the scriptures, which says the whole world was born through the *tapasya* – austerity – of Prajapati. That only means that nothing can be made without some kind of sacrifice (*tapasya* is also "sacrifice"). Unless you give up something, you cannot find something else.

"He was born before the waters": this, again, is the cosmological story of how the whole world was created from the waters. In fact, "Narayana" means "the vehicle in the deep waters": *ayana* means "vehicle"; in the *nara* "deep waters".

That ancient Being, from the beginning, having entered the secret place of the heart, dwells in the body made of five elements and looks forth through these beings. When I say, "I look," it is the Supreme Being who is looking forth. When I am identified with my individual Self, I am separate; I look and I see only a few things. Now, you are also identified with your individual Self and so you also see a few things. So do all the people in this world, who look through their eyes and their individual self.

Therefore, the Supreme Self who is in all, sees everything, all at once, because He is seeing through you, He is seeing through me and through everyone else. So This Being is indeed That Being.

SHLOKA 7

yaa praanena sambhavaty ya aditir devataamayi
guhaam pravishya tishthantim yaa bhutebhir vyajaayata
etat vai tat

"She, who rises with the 'life-force' – *prana* – that *aditi,* the soul of the gods, the first-born who was created with the elements, has entered the secret place of the heart and dwells there. This is verily That."

Here the Supreme Being is called "She" instead of "He" as earlier, meaning *aditi,* "the soul of the gods". *Aditi* means "unbound" or "boundless". She, who rises with life, that unbound *aditi,* the soul of the gods, has manifested with the elements as the life-force – *prana* – and has entered the secret place of the heart. This *aditi,* the soul of the gods, the first-born, who was born with all the beings, is no other than That Supreme Being. "This is indeed That."

SHLOKA 8

aranyor nihito jaata vedaa garbha iva subhrito garbhinnibhih
dive diva eedyo jaagrivadbhih havishmadbhir manushyebhir agnih
etad vai tat

"That omniscient *agni,* like the well-protected embryo in pregnant woman, is lodged hidden in the two fire sticks; He is adored daily by the watchful men, who offer oblations to the sacrificial fire. This is verily That."

Agni is associated with sticks because in ancient times, when they wanted a fire, they rubbed two sticks together and out of that came the fire. So it is a symbol of that which is hidden, which can manifest at any time, from any place. So *agni,* hidden in the sticks, is also compared to the embryo, hidden in the well-protected womb of pregnant women.

That means, That Supreme Being stays hidden in the secret place, like an embryo in the womb and the unmanifest fire in the sticks. That *agni* should be adored daily by the watchful people, who offer It oblations, as This is indeed That.

Every day, human beings should adore That inner Being, hidden like fire within, and offer oblations unto that inner Being. "Offer oblations" means sacrifice everything else to the understanding of that inner Fire, which is also called the Nachiketas-fire.

SHLOKA 9

yatah cha udeti sooryo astam yatra cha gachhati
tam devaas sarve arpitaas tadu naatyeti kas chana
etad vai tat

"That, from where the sun rises and to where it goes to rest – in It are all the gods founded and no god goes beyond That. This is verily That."

The sun, from where it rises and to where it sets, means the universe, the entire cosmos, everything, is rooted in That Supreme Being, including the gods. It means that there is nothing that is not in the ambit of that Supreme Being and none can go beyond It. It covers everything.

Next, the *rishi* of the Upanishad gives poetic descriptions of It, one by one, so that nothing is left out.

SHLOKA 10

yat eva iha tat amutra yat amutra tat anviha
mrityoh sa mrityum aapnoti ya iha naana iva pashyati

"Whatever is here, is also there; what is there, is also here. Whoever perceives 'the many' here goes from death to death."

That means, That Supreme Being is all-pervading – "whatever is here, that is also there". *Isha vasyam idam sarvam* – "that Supreme Being pervades everything here". There is no place where It is not – It is here, It is also there.

"Whoever perceives 'the many' here goes from death to death" – What the Upanishad means is that when one realises that in "the many" that you see, there is only the Supreme Being, then, one is safe. Otherwise, one goes from death to death.

Now, "death to death" could mean, metaphysically, that one is born again and again. It could also mean that one tries to enjoy one's desires again and again and because one enjoys and then gets sorrow when it is finished, that is like death. But then, one looks for more enjoyment again and again, and suffers – that is also "death to death."

The one who sees the Unity as the essential Self, has no death because he is always in that tranquility.

SHLOKA 11

manasa eva idam aaptavyam na iha naanaasti kin chana
mrityoh sa mrityum gacchati ya iha naana iva pashyati

"By mind alone is That to be attained. There is no variety here, it is all One. Whoever perceives variety goes from death to death."

The Self is to be attained only by the mind. It cannot be obtained by anything else. There is no variety and the one who perceives variety, goes from death to death. Whoever perceives Unity as the essence of all beings remains anchored in the inner Self. It is to be attained only through the mind; there is no other way. One can only reach It through thinking about It, by trying to understand It; not by reaching for It through the senses.

SHLOKA 12

angushtha maatrah purusho madhya aatmani tishthati
ishaano bhoota bhavyasya na tato vijigupsate
etad vai tat

"That *purusha,* of the size of a thumb, resides in the middle of the body. After knowing Him, who is the Lord of the past and the future, one does not move away from Him anymore. This is verily That."

That Supreme Being, the *purusha,* is "of the size of the thumb". This is a figurative and poetic expression to indicate that It is small and very subtle, remaining hidden inside. It does not mean that the Supreme Being is residing inside, looking like a thumb!

That inner Being resides in the "middle of the body", in the inner recesses of one's consciousness, meaning in the "heart" which is the centre of consciousness – not the physical heart. After knowing that Supreme Being, who resides in the heart, who is the Lord of the past and the future, one does not move away from Him anymore because one has understood one's true identity in Being. This "thumb-sized" *purusha* is no other than That Supreme Being. There is no difference. This is That.

SHLOKA 13

angushtha maatrah purusho jyotir iva adhoomakah
eeshaano bhoota bhavyasya sa evaadya sa u shvah
etad vai tat

"That *purusha,* of the size of a thumb, is like a flame without smoke. He is the Lord of the past and the future. He is the same today and also the same tomorrow. This verily is That."

That Supreme Person, the *purusha,* residing as *atma* in the individual, in the middle of the body, of the size of a thumb, "is like a flame without smoke". That means It is Self-existing. Any flame, which has been lit from outside, has some smoke. Here, It is a Self-sustaining flame; therefore, It does not have smoke. He is the unchanging Lord, who is the same today and the same tomorrow. There is no difference. This *purusha* is verily That Supreme Being.

SHLOKA 14

yathodakam durge vrishtham parvateshu vidhaavati
evam dharmaan prithak pashyams taan eva anuvidhaavati

"As rain water on a hill top flows down the hill sides in various streams, so he who sees the various things of the world as different, verily runs after them, distracted."

He who sees the various things of the world as different, runs after them distracted. He goes behind each stream, thinking this stream is different from the other, and he is exhausted trying to find the source. The source is One, coming from the top, like the rain. He does not know the underlying unity of the Self, the Supreme Being, and sees the world as different.

SHLOKA 15

yathodakam shuddhe shuddham aasiktam taadrig eva bhavati
evam muner vijaanata aatmaa bhavati gautama

"O Gautama, as pure water poured into pure water becomes the same water, so the seer, who has the understanding of the inner Self, becomes One."

The seer, who has the understanding of the Self and knows the unity of the *atman,* becomes one with the Supreme Being. There is no more a separate identity for that Being as he is merged with the Supreme Being – just as pure water poured into pure water merges and becomes one.

CHAPTER 5

The *rishi* of the Upanishad gives another beautiful description:

SHLOKA 1

puram ekaadasha dvaaram ajasya avakra chetasah
anushthaaya na shochati vimuktahs cha vimuchyate
etad vai tat

"The unborn, of uncrooked Intelligence, sits in the city of eleven gates, ruling. Having known That, one does not grieve any more and being freed, is free indeed. This verily is That Supreme."

Most of us have heard of "the city of nine gates" which means the human body with its *nava dwaras* or "nine openings": seven in the head and two lower ones. Here, two more have been added, which shows a shift to the practical application of *yoga*. In the *yogic* parlance, there are eleven *dwaras* in the body. Apart from these *nava dwaras*, there are two more important *dwaras*: one is at the *nabhi* or navel, from where creation comes up and the other *dwara* is at the top of the head, called *brahmarandhra*. You can feel it at the top of the head of a new-born child – there is a soft part there, where there is a pulse. After a while, it becomes hard. That is called *brahmarandhra* by the yogis: that, by which the *prana* exits.This applies only to great souls, not for everybody.

So this body is the city of eleven gates. In that city sits the "unborn, uncrooked Intelligence" – the Self, which is not born, though we think It is born, which is not crooked, but straight and direct and has not been caught in the crookedness of our usual intellect, by which generally, we seek "the pleasant" and not "the good". We are so caught up by the senses, that even though we think we are thinking straight, we are not – we are only thinking of satisfying the senses in some way. The moment somebody says something which may not be pleasant for the senses, we think it is nonsense!

So, knowing That direct Intelligence, the Self, the unborn, who sits ruling in the city of eleven gates, the body, one does not grieve any more and being freed, is free indeed. This *atman*, the Self in the city, is verily That Supreme Being.

SHLOKA 2

hamsah shuchishat vasur antarikshasat
hotaa vedishat atithir duronnasat
nrishat varasat ritasat vyomasat abjaa gojaa
ritajaa adrijaa ritam brihat

"That Supreme Being is the swan (the sun) moving in the sky; the pervader in space (the air); the priest who offers (the fire) in the altar; the guest in the sacrificial jar. He dwells in men, He dwells in gods, He resides in the sacrificial rites, He is in the all-pervading sky. He is born of water, He sprang from the earth, He is there in the mountains. He is the Supreme, the Great Being."

This is a beautiful description of the all-pervading Supreme Being, who is in everything that exists. Even if you don't know the meaning of the Sanskrit words, the sound is beautiful. It means: That Supreme Being is "the swan in the sky" – some *acharyas* have also interpreted this "swan" to mean "the sun in the sky" which rises and sets. But I think if you can forget the sun, and can see a white swan gliding up suddenly, and as it goes up, covers the entire horizon. As it flies, it is as if it has left the heaviness of the earth and is afloat, high up there – it is a wonderful feeling!

It also means that the swan in the sky is like the sun in the sky. It is That Supreme Being, who is the sun in the sky. He is the air that pervades space, He is the sacrificial fire, He is the priest who offers at the altar, He is the guest at every sacrifice. He is the one who eats, while we eat. He dwells in man and in the gods. He dwells in rites and rhythm *hrita* can also be "order" or "rhythm". He pervades the sky, the earth, the mountains and the water. He is the Great, all-pervading Being in everything that is.

Then comes a description of how It is connected to the practice of *yoga.*

SHLOKA 3

oordhvam praanam unnayaty apaanam pratyag asyati
madhye vaamanam aaseenam vishve devaa upaasate

"He leads the in-breath, *praana,* upwards and casts the out-breath, *apaana,* downwards. That Little Being, *vaamana,* who is seated in the middle, all the gods adore."

That Supreme Being, seated in the heart, is called *vaamana* or "dwarf". When a person reaches the stage where he understands that

Little Being is within himself, even the gods adore Him. And who is He? He is the one who leads the in-breath upwards and He casts the out-breath downwards.

Generally, we are not aware of this, but from the time we are born till the time we die, the breath is moving up and down. The moment it stops, we are dead. We don't ask the lungs to breathe; the process goes on by itself and when it stops, we reach the end.

We can live without food for sometime; we can live without water also, for quite sometime, but we cannot live without breath for even a few minutes. So it is one of the most important sources that sustain our system. Therefore, it is called the Life-Giver or Life-Force, *praana*. The moment it is gone, there is nothing left.

So the *praana*, which goes in and out is very important. And there is some Intelligence which operates this going in and out, although we are not aware of It. There are other functions also in the body, which work without our knowledge. Circulation works without our knowledge, digestion works without our knowledge. The heart beats without our asking it to beat – so also the breath goes in and out. But, there is a difference here. Breath happens to be one function, which, although is involuntary all the time, can also be voluntarily controlled, if we want.

Therefore, breath is the link to that Intelligence, which is always controlling it. I hope you can grasp what I am trying to say. As you begin to control your breath, or become aware of your breath and try to change the pattern, you are moving closer to that Intelligence, which is always adjusting its pattern. It is also one's practical experience that when you watch and become aware of your breath, the breath slows down ultimately. And when it slows down, there is absolute quietitude. From there, one connects to meditation. So, the breath is especially mentioned here.

SHLOKA 4

asya visramsamaanasya shareerasthasya dehinah
dehaad vimuchyamaanasya kima atra parishishyate
etad vai tat

"When the embodied Self that dwells within the body, slips off and is released from the body, what remains then? This is verily That."

So when the *praana,* the Life-Force, leaves the body, it becomes of no use. When the *atman* is released from the body – nothing else but only That Supreme Being is left.

SHLOKA 5

na praanena na apaanena martyo jeevati kash chana
itarena tu jeevanti yasminn etaav upaashritau

"No mortal ever lives by the in-breath, *praana* or by the out-breath, *apaana;* but lives by something different, on whom these depend."

SHLOKA 6

hanta te idam pravakshyaami guhyam brahma sanaatanam
yathaa cha maranam praapya aatmaa bhavati gautama

"O Gautama, I shall explain to you the mystery of the eternal Brahman and what happens to the Self after reaching Death."

Yama says to Nachiketas, who is called Gautama, "I shall explain to you what happens to the soul after death." When the body dies, we think we are dead. What really happens? Yama explains:

SHLOKA 7

yonim anye prapadyante shareeratvaaya dehinah
sthaannum anye anusamyanti yathaa karma yathaa shrutam

"Some souls enter a womb for embodiment, according to their deeds, according to their desires – others go to stations immovable."

After the body dies, some souls enter a womb to have a body according to their deeds and their desires. What they desire that they gain, and therefore, it is said, that whatever one's mind is fixed on, during the last stages of one's life, that one attains. But, it cannot be done in the last minute. One must think about it from the beginning, otherwise it is not possible.

There is this old story about this extreme miser, who wanted to think of God, as he was passing away. So he was fixing his mind on God, but just at the moment before he passed away, suddenly he turned and saw that the wick in the oil lamp, which was burning, was a little forward – oil was being wasted! So he told his sons, "Push the wick in." That was the last thing he thought of and so he was supposed to have been reborn as an oil-seller! So, according to their deeds, according to their desires and according to their thoughts, souls come back into a womb for embodiment.

SHLOKA 8

ya esha supteshu jaagarti kaamam kaamam purusho nirmimaanah
tad eva shukram tad brahma tad eva amrutam uchyate
tasmin lokaah shritaah sarve tad u naatyeti kash chana
etad vai tat

"That Person, the *purusha,* who is awake in those who sleep, shaping desire after desire, That one is, indeed, the pure, That is the Brahman and That is also called the immortal. In It, all the worlds rest and no one goes beyond It. This verily is That."

This means, That *purusha,* the Self, who is awake even when one is in sound sleep, who watches the shaping of desire after desire in the dream state, but is not involved in it, who is the Witness of all that is happening; That Self is indeed the pure Self, That Self is the Brahman, the Supreme Self, the immortal one. All the worlds rest in It and no one can go beyond It, which means, even the *devas* cannot go beyond It.

That is why, they say, a human being is very important. When a human being reaches a high spiritual stature, even the gods have to bow down to him. In the Ramayana, when Ravana took the boon that no *devas* could kill him, he forgot to mention human beings. So the Supreme Being, according to the Ramayana, had to come in human form and kill Ravana, who could do nothing about it.

So, it is important to use the life that we have gained and not waste it.

SHLOKA 9

agnir yatha ekah bhuvanam pravishto roopam roopam
pratiroopo babhoova
ekas tathaa sarva bhootaantaraatmaa roopam roopam
pratiroopo bahis cha

"As fire, which is one, having entered the world becomes varied according to the shapes which it occupies, so also the One Self within all beings becomes varied according to whatever It enters; but It also exists outside them."

Fire, as it is, does not have any shape. But, when it burns something, say a tree trunk, and when it is finished, you see a charred tree trunk. So, depending on the object it burns, it assumes that form.

So also, the One Self becomes varied, according to whatever forms It enters. But It also exists outside them, without them, without change, like fire. The original fire is always the original fire. When the fire enters the tree trunk, it burns it and then it is gone. But the fire now has no shape. In the same way, even though the Supreme Self enters different *roopas,* or forms, It also exists outside that *roopa.*

SHLOKA 10

vaayur yathaa eko bhuvanam pravishto roopam roopam
pratiroopo babhoova
ekah tathaa sarva bhoota antaraatma roopam roopam
pratiroopo bahis cha

"As air, which is one air, having entered this world acquires different shapes according to the objects that it enters, so also, the One Supreme Self, within all beings, becomes varied according to whatever It enters. And, It also exists outside."

For example, there is air in this empty cup, and it is in the shape of the cup. But, apart from being in that cup, it also exists outside. In the same way, the Supreme Self is within all beings and also exists outside them.

SHLOKA 11

suryo yathaa sarva lokasya chakshur
na lipyate chaakshushair baahya doshaih
ekas tathaa sarva bhootaantaraatmaa
na lipyate loka duhkhena baahyah

"Just as the sun, the eye of the whole world, is not defiled by the faults seen by it, even so, the one *atman* within all beings is not tainted by the sorrows of the world."

The sun rises. Due of the light of the sun, everything is seen, but the sun is not affected by the faults of that which is seen. Even so, the Self within all beings is not tainted by the sorrows of the world because although it appears that He is in the sorrow, He is really outside it.

SHLOKA 12

eko vashee sarva bhootaantaraatmaa
ekam beejam bahudhaa yah karoti
tam aatmastham ye anupashyanti dheerah
teshaam sukham shaashvatam netareshaam

"That One controller, the inner Self of all things, makes His one form into many forms. Those wise who perceive Him as only One, abiding in the soul, get eternal bliss – nobody else gets it."

The wise who know the Supreme Being – who makes His One form into many different forms and abides within as the Self, the *atman* – get bliss. The one caught in differences is stuck in sorrow, whereas, the one who sees unity of being, is in happiness.

SHLOKA 13

nityo anityanaam chetanash chetanaanaam
eko bahoonaam yo vidadhaati kaamaan

tam aatmastham ye anupashyanti dheerah
teshaam shaantih shaashvatee na itareshaam

"He is the eternal One, who is the basis of all that is transient and changing; the One, who is the conscious amidst the different levels of consciousness; the One, who grants the desires of the many. Those wise men who perceive Him as being in their own soul – to them is eternal peace and to no other."

SHLOKA 14

tad etad iti manyante anirdeshyam paramam sukham
katham nu tad vijaaneeyaam kimu bhaati vibhaati vaa

"This is That Supreme Self which the wise recognise as the ineffable Supreme Bliss. How can I come to know It? Does It shine or does It not shine in the reflection?"

That Supreme Self, which the wise recognise as Bliss; how am I supposed to recognise It as the eternal, blissful Self, which is in me? Does It shine by Itself or does It need anything else to shine? How can I find that out? Am I a reflection of That Supreme Self? Is It luminous?

The answer follows, describing the Self-effulgence of *atman*. In That Supreme Self:

SHLOKA 15

na tatra suryo bhaati na chandra taarakam
na imaah vidyuto bhaanti kutah ayam agnih
tam eva bhaantam anubhaati sarvam
tasya bhaasaa sarvam idam vibhaati

"The sun does not shine there, nor do the moon and the stars; nor does the lightning shine. How then, can this fire? Everything shines only after That Shining Light. It is His shining that illumines all this."

That means neither the sun nor the moon nor the stars – which are the heavenly bodies that we know of – nor the lightning and much less the fire, are needed to illuminate this Supreme Being. This Original Being shines first, and from Him shines everything else. Therefore, He need not be illumined either by the sun or the moon or by electricity, or by anything else.

It is just to show that this Supreme Reality, which the Upanishad is talking about, is not illumined by anything, but is the Source of all illumination – It is the Source of all Light.

CHAPTER 6

There is a *shloka* in the 15th chapter of the Bhagwad Gita that talks about the "upside-down tree". Here, the Upanishad also mentions it:

SHLOKA 1

oordhvamoolah avaakshaakha eshah ashvatthah sanaatanah
tad eva shukram tad brahma tad evaamritam uchyate
tasmin lokaah shritaah sarve tad u naatyeti kash chana
etad vai tat

"There is a tree with the roots above and branches below – the ancient Ashwatha tree. That is the pure tree, that is the Brahman, that indeed is also called the immortal. In it, all the worlds rest and no one goes beyond it. This verily is That."

The Upanishad is not trying to say that the Supreme Being is an upside-down Ashwatha tree! It is a figurative expression of trying to explain that, as far as the teaching of the Supreme Self is concerned, it is not from the "particular" to the "universal", but from the "universal" to the "particular"- it is not inductive reasoning.

The roots are up and the branches are down below – this means that the beginning is invisible and what is seen as the manifest is visible. Therefore, seeing the visible, one begins to wonder what is the invisible, which is the root of all this.

The branches and leaves do not satisfy the wise, who want to find out what the root is. The whole tree with its root is the Supreme Being and the branches spread out, is the world that we see – the visible world. It is an illustration of the Supreme Being pervading this entire universe.

Although the essence is in the roots above, it also means,"as above, so below", "That above, This below": *etad vai tat.* What we see here is the manifest, and what is above is the Unmanifest. However here, the Unmanifest is the root and the manifest, the branches. This is the meaning of *oordhvamoolam* – the *moolaa* is up, the root is up, the branches are below.

SHLOKA 2

yad idam kin cha jagat sarvam praana ejati nihshritam
mahad bhayam vajram udyatam ye etad vidur r amritaas
te bhavanti

"The *prana* being present, the whole universe comes out of Him and vibrates within Him. He is a great terror like the raised thunderbolt. Those who know this become immortal."

SHLOKA 3

bhayaad asya agnis tapati bhayaat tapati suryah
bhayaad indras cha vaayus cha mrityur dhaavati
panchamah

"For fear of Him the Fire burns; for fear of Him shines the Sun; for fear of Him do Indra, Vayu and Death, the five, proceed with their respective functions."

SHLOKA 4

iha ched ashakad boddhum praak shareerasya visrasah
tatah sargeshu lokeshu shareeratvaaya kalpate

"If one is able to realise that Brahman here, before the fall of the body, one becomes free from the bondage of the world; if not, one has to take body again in the worlds of creation."

SHLOKA 5

yathaa aadarshe tathaa aatmani
yathaa svapne tathaa pitrloke
yatha aapsu pareeva dadrishe tathaa gandharva loke
chaayaa tapayor iva brahma loke

"Brahman is seen in the Self as one sees oneself in a mirror; in the world of manes, as one perceives oneself in dream; in the world of Gandharvas, as one's reflection is seen in the water; in the world of Brahma, as light and shade."

SHLOKA 6

indriyaannaam prithag bhaavam udayaastamayau cha yat
prithag utpadyamaanaanam matvaa dheero na shochati

"The wise one, having known the distinct nature of the senses, which are separately produced, as well as about their rising and setting, grieves not."

SHLOKA 7

indriyebhyah param mano manasah sattvam uttamam
sattvaad adhi mahaan aatmaa mahatah avyaktam uttamam

"Beyond the senses is the mind, beyond the mind is the intellect, beyond the intellect is the Great *atman*. Superior to the Great *atman* is the Unmanifest."

SHLOKA 8

avyaktaat tu parah purusho vyaapakah alinga eva cha
yam jnyaatvaa muchyate jantur amritatvam cha gacchati

"Beyond the Unmanifest, is the *purusha,* That Being, who is all-pervading, who is without any marks, knowing whom, a human is liberated and goes to life eternal."

Beyond that which is not manifest, which is the root of the tree, is the all-pervading *purusha,* who has no *linga,* meaning he has no distinctive mark on Him anywhere. That means He cannot be marked and He is "without blemish" – *nirmala.* There is nothing which can stick to Him. Knowing Him, man is liberated.

SHLOKA 9

na sandrishe tishthat roopam asya
na chakshushaa pashyati kashchana inam
hridaa maneeshaa manasa abhiklupto
ya etad vidur amiutaas te bhavanti

"He does not stand in the field of our vision. No one sees Him with these eyes. Through the heart, through the mind, through thought alone He is apprehended. Those who know Him become immortal."

That Supreme Being cannot be seen by our ordinary faculties of sensation, by our ordinary field of vision. "Field of vision" does not mean the eyes only, but all our sensory organs and apparatus. This means that He cannot be seen through our sensory organs. With our sensory apparatus we cannot even see bacteria – we need a microscope! Only because we cannot see, we cannot say it does not exist.

In the same way, the inner Self cannot be seen by our ordinary sense organs. He can be seen and apprehended through the heart, *hridaya,* in the inner recesses of the mind and those who know Him become immortal.

SHLOKA 10

yadaa pancha avatishthante jnyaanaani manasaa saha
buddhhish cha na vicheshtati taam aahuh paramaam gatim

"When the five senses, together with the mind, cease from all activity and the intelligence itself does not stir, that is the highest state, they say."

Having seen the futility of trying to understand the Supreme Being through the senses, and, having seen the futility of enjoying that which can end at any time; having completely understood this, and having listened to the Upanishad and knowing that one's inner Self resides within, when one no more attempts to achieve anything outside and settles down quietly, when the mind becomes absolutely quiet, when even the intelligence does not stir, but remains steady in itself, one is at the highest state.

SHLOKA 11

taam yogam iti manyante sthiraam indriya dhaarannaam
apramattas tadaa bhavati yogo hi prabha vaapyayau

"This state, where there is steady control of all the senses, is what is called *yoga.* Then one becomes undisturbed from the practice of *yoga.* In that steadiness, one remains without stirring."

That state, where everything has become quiet and does not stir and the *yogi* has steady control of all the senses – that, they consider to be *yoga.* "Control of all the senses" means the senses have become absolutely quiet and one remains without stirring.

SHLOKA 12

naiva vaachaa na manasaa praaptum shakyo na
chakshushaa
asti iti bruvato anyatra katham tad upalabhyate

"Not by speech, not by mind, not by sight, can It be apprehended. How then can It be apprehended, except from those who say, 'It is'?"

The Supreme Being exists – so the sages say. The only way to comprehend the Supreme Being is to understand that It is. As Plato states,

"There are two eternal things in this universe: one is, and is 'never-becoming'; the other is not, but is 'ever-becoming.'"

So, when one is free from that which "is not, but is ever-becoming" which is our mind, and one remains in that which "is, and is never-becoming", then that is the state called *asti.* In fact, in the Vedantasutras, Vyaasa describes the Supreme Being as *asti bhaati priya. Asti* is That which is, without any movement whatsoever, in Its Being – essential "Being-ness". *Bhaati* is Consciousness, Self-effulgence. *Priya* is that because of which one understands what is known as Love.

SHLOKA 13

asti ity eva upalabdhavyah tattva bhaavena cha ubhayoh
asti ity eva upalabdhasya tattva bhaavah praseedati

"It should be apprehended only as existent in Its real nature. When It is apprehended as existent, Its real nature becomes clear."

In the beginning, the only thing one can do is to understand that It is only pure existence, without any movement. As you keep contemplating on this fact and going deeper and deeper, then you will understand what that real Self is.

Why does it take time to understand what that real Self is? It is because there are still some conditionings in the mind that stop us from looking at It clearly.

And what are these conditionings of the mind?

SHLOKA 14

yadaa sarve pramuchyante kaamaa ye asya hrudi shritaah
atha martyah amrutah bhavaty atra brahma samashnute

"When all the desires that dwell within the heart are cast away, then a mortal becomes immortal even here, and attains that Brahman."

How does one begin? One cannot, obviously, begin by casting off all desires. That is not possible, nor is it reasonable to do so. When all desires become united into a strong, single desire for the understanding of that Supreme Being, and one sees the impermanence of fulfilment of the desires of this world, then one becomes steady and begins to think of that Supreme Being as pure existence. Gradually, the hold of the senses gets loosened and they drop away and one reaches that Supreme Brahman.

SHLOKA 15

yadaa sarve prabhidyante hrudayasyacha granthayah
atha martyah amruto bhavaty etaavad anushaasanam

"When all the knots that fetter the heart are cut asunder; then a mortal becomes immortal. Thus far is the teaching."

When all desires are cast away and the knots that fetter the heart are cut, then a mortal becomes immortal. Otherwise, he is still caught in individual existence. Then the Upanishad confesses: "Thus far is the teaching." Beyond this, we cannot say anything. All that we can say is that this is the limit to which we can speak about the unspeakable.

Then the *rishi* of the Upanishad gives a very *yogic* description about the *naadis,* or subtle nerves that come out of the heart, the centre of one's being:

SHLOKA 16

shatam cha ekaa cha hrudayasya naadyahs
taasaam murdhaanam api nihshruta ekaa
tayaa urdvam aayan amrutatvam eti
vishvank anyah utkramanne bhavanti

"A hundred and one are the *naadis* that come out of the heart. One of them leads to the crown of the head. Going upwards through that, one becomes immortal. The other *naadis* are for going in other directions, after death."

Now, this *yogic* description has not been covered by the earlier Upanishads. In the later ones, we have the Yoga Upanishads which talk about this. But in the earlier Upanishads, these are not mentioned.

According to *yoga,* our system has many *naadis,* the subtle nerves, of which the *ida* and the *pingala* are the two main ones. The major one is the *sushumna naadi,* which is supposed to run straight, from the heart to the head.

It is not an anatomical system – you cannot find it if you open up a dead body. You can find the spinal cord, but you cannot find any *naadis* going up and down. You can see some nerve centres and plexuses of the nervous system – the ganglion chain and the central nervous system with the spine and the brain and so on – but, you cannot actually see the *naadis,* as described, with the *chakras.* These are basically psychic centres. So they are talking about that which we cannot go into details here, of the different *naadis* that come out of the heart – heart, meaning the centre of one's consciousness, not the physical heart.

The major *naadi* that goes up from the heart to the crown of the head is the *sushumna naadi.* When the *prana* leaves the body through that, then one becomes immortal. When it leaves the body through the other *naadis,* then one goes in various directions, after death.

The centre in the head is considered to be the highest – this is known as *brahmarandhra* in *yogic* parlance. When all of one's thoughts and energy are concentrated on the highest centre, then, all the energies are flowing through that *naadi* towards the Supreme Being. And when thought is flowing through the lower centres, then it is absorbed in other activities, which bring the soul back again and again to this earth, into this circuit of pleasure and pain.

SHLOKA 17

angushtha maatrah purushah antar aatma
sadaa janaanaam hridaye sannivishthah
tam svaacchareeraat pravrihen munnjaad iva ishikaam dhairyena
tam vidyaat shukram amritam tam vidyaat
shukram amritam iti

"The Person, the *purusha,* of the size of the thumb, the inner Self, always abides in the hearts of men. Him, one should draw out firmly from the body, as the wind drawn out from the reed. That Supreme Being – one should know as the pure, the immortal. That Supreme Being – one should know as the pure, the immortal."

That Supreme Being resides in the innermost Self, in the hearts of all beings. He should be drawn out from the body firmly. If you are complacent, you cannot draw It out. You should draw It out from the body, with firmness, with alertness, with attention, with understanding, as the wind is drawn out forcibly from the reed.

This also has *yogic* connotations. Just as you would forcibly draw out the wind through a tube, so also, the practicing *yogi* draws out the *prana* upwards, through the *sushumna naadi,* which is supposed to be shaped like a reed.

It also means that all of one's energies, all of one's thoughts, everything, should be completely aligned to understanding that Supreme Self. When that is done one experiences the Supreme Self, the pure, the immortal.

SHLOKA 18

mrityproktaam nachiketo atha labdhvaa
vidyaam etaam yoga vidhim cha kritsnam
brahma praapto virajah abhood vimrityur
anyah api evam yo vid adhyaatmam eva

"Then Nachiketas, having gained this knowledge declared by Death and also the rules of *yoga,* attained that Supreme Brahman and became free from passion and therefore, free from Death. So may others, who know thus the inner Self, be free!"

There is definitely a description of some kind of *yogic* practice here. Just as Nachiketas became free through understanding this may anyone else, who has given attention to it, become as free as Nachiketas and reach immortality.

This is the end of the Katha Upanishad – the reading of the Upanishad, not the end of the *katha.* The *katha,* or story, has just started. Each one has to work out the story by himself or herself!

Aum shantih shantih shantihi!

Prashna Upanishad

Having come to a theoretical understanding of the Reality behind the illusionary perception that the Upanishads speak about, I would like to go into a proper Upanishad and see how the great *rishis,* the teachers of the Upanishads, handled this question of self-discovery or self-realisation. This is the knowledge of the Self, which is also the knowledge of the all-pervading consciousness.

Let us take up the Prashna Upanishad, which is not a very popular Upanishad. It should be, because, it is an Upanishad that questions. The word *prashna* means "question". So it is an Upanishad which does not accept, but questions before accepting. That should be the hallmark of any enquiry – not to believe just because somebody said so, but to question, to ask. All great things have been achieved by asking and questioning, not otherwise.

The Prashna Upanishad belongs to the Atharva Veda. It has six sections which contain six questions putforth to a great *rishi* by his disciples, who were all seekers of the Supreme Reality. They wanted to know about the ultimate cause of everything – about the powers that support creation; about the origin of *praana,* the Life Energy; about the nature of the human being and the waking, dream and deep sleep states; about the sound *aum* which is chanted; about the Supreme Being, the Person, and its relationship with the world and so on.

Most of the Upanishads begin with an invocation. The invocation is a prayer to the Gods to keep everything in order – body and mind – so that one may examine the universal questions and go deep into the understanding of Truth.

The invocation in the Prashna Upanishad is:

Aum bhadram karnebhih shrunuyaama devaah
bhadram pashyema-akshabhir yajatraah
sthirair angais tushtuvaamsas tanoobhih
vyashema devahitam yad aayuh

svasti na indro vruddhashravaah
svasti nah pushaa vishvavedaah
svasti nas taarkshyo arishta nemih
svasti no brihaspatir dadhaatu
Aum shaantih shaantih shaantih

"Aum, May we O Gods, hear what is auspicious with our ears;

O ye, who are worthy of worship, may we see with our eyes, what is auspicious;

May we enjoy the life allotted to us by the Gods, offering praise, with our bodies strong and our limbs strong;

May Indra, of increasing glory, bestow prosperity on us;

May Pushan, the nourisher of all, bestow prosperity on us;

May Tarkshyah, of unobstructed path bestow prosperity on us;

May Brihaspati bestow prosperity on us.

Aum, peace, peace, peace!"

QUESTION ONE

The six sons of great *rishis*, all seekers of Truth, approach the revered *rishi* Pippalaada, wanting to know all about Brahman, the Supreme Reality, and the created universe.

SHLOKA 1

sukesha cha bhaaradvaaja shaibyash cha satyakaamah sauryaayani cha
gaargyah kausalysh cha shvalaayano bhaargavo vaidarbhih kabandhii
kaatyaayanah te haite brahma paarah brahma nishthaah
param brahmaanveshamaanaa esha ha vai tat sarvam vakshyati iti
te ha samit paanayo bhagavantam pipalaadam upasannaah.

"Sukesha, son of Bhaaradvaaja; Satyakaama, son of Shibi; Gargya, the grandson of Surya; Kausalya, son of Ashvala; Bhaargava of the Vidarbha clan and Kabandhin, son of Katya – all these, indeed devoted to Brahman and seeking to know the Highest Brahman, approach the revered Pippalada with sacrificial fuel in their hands, thinking that he would explain all that to them."

These young men, sons of *rishis* themselves and seekers of the Highest Truth, approach Pippalada, the great revered *rishi,* wanting to know what the Supreme Reality, the Brahman, is. Thinking that he would explain everything, they approach with *samit* or sacrificial fuel, in their hands.

That means, to find the Truth, one has to sacrifice the "untruth". One has to be intent and make it a one-pointed search, no matter what stands as an obstacle. One should be ready to sacrifice it, in the search for knowledge. That "sacrifice" is the "sacrificial fuel" in their hands. So, intent on understanding the Supreme and ready to sacrifice anything to do so, they approach the great *rishi* Pippalada.

SHLOKA 2

taan ha sa rishir uvaacha bhooya eva tapasaa
brahmacharyena shraddhayaa samvatsaram samvatsyatha
yathaa kaamam prashnaan pricchata
yadi vijnaasyaamah sarvam ha vo vakshyaama iti

"The *rishi,* the seer, said to them, 'Live with me for a year with austerity, chastity and faith and then ask me questions according to your desire. If I know, I shall indeed tell you all that.'"

Pippalada wanted to prepare them to understand the highest Truth. He said to them, "Live with me here, for a year". That means, to lead a simple life and not get caught up in the indulgence of luxury.

"Live here in this beautiful forest with me with austerity, chastity and faith. Stick to the truth, be chaste, be pure. Have faith that the answer will come, after you have lived with me for one full year." That is the preliminary preparation for the understanding of Truth, which we are not prepared to do – we just want to find the Truth. It is necessary to become qualified to enquire.

Pippalada does not presuppose that he knows the answers; he does not have ready answers. He did not say, "I will then answer them." Instead, he said, "If I know, I shall indeed tell you all that."

After the seekers thus lived for a year, after they had followed the instructions of the *rishi* Pippalada, they approached him with their questions. It is indeed "Prashna" Upanishad -"the questioning" Upanishad.

Kabandhin, son of the *rishi* Katya, asked the first question about creation:

SHLOKA 3

atha kabandhii kaatyaayana upetya papraccha
bhagavan kuto ha vaa imaah prajaah prajaayante iti

"Kabandhin, son of Katya, first approached the *rishi* and said, 'Bhagavan, venerable Sir, from where have all the creatures been born?'"

SHLOKA 4

tasmai sa hovaacha prajaa kaamo vai prajaapatih sa tapah atapyata sa
tapas taptvaa sa mithunam utpaadayate rayim cha praanam cha ity etau
me bahudhaa prajaah karishyata iti

"To him the *rishi* said, 'Prajaapati, the creator, the lord of creation, had this desire to multiply. He performed *tapasya.* After he had performed austerities, he produced a pair – Matter, or *rayih,* and Life, or *praana,* thinking that they would produce creatures for him in various ways."

That means, austerity, or *tapasya,* is required for any kind of multiplication, for growth. Even Prajapati, the Lord of Creation, who desired to multiply, to have off-spring, performed austerities.

So, the first principal of creativity, the Creator, through austerity, produced a pair. What are they? Matter and Life: Matter, which is non-living and inanimate, and Life, which is the Energy that animates it. And, between Matter and Life, was produced all that exists in the universe.

SHLOKA 5

aadityo ha vai praanah rayir eva chandramaah rayir vaa etat sarvam yan moortam cha amoortam cha tasmaat moortir eva rayih

"The Sun indeed is Life – *praana*; and Matter, *rayih,* is the Moon. Then is formed whatever is with form and the formless. Therefore, whatever there is, is itself Matter."

The *rishi* goes on to explain what this Life is, what this *praana* is, and its different variations and how it is in different forms. "The Sun indeed is Life – *praana*" because it is the Sun that causes photosynthesis, it is the Sun that makes life. If there is no Sun for some days, there will be no agriculture, no growth, nothing. It is the Sun that gives light and heat.

"Matter is the Moon" because the Moon is identified with coolness. We have the cool light of the Moon and the hot light of the Sun. The Moon is feminine with its cool, silvery light, and the Sun is masculine with its hot, fiery light. So when virility or the hot, glowing light of the Sun, the Life, unites with the cool light of the Moon, the Matter, "then is formed whatever is with form and what is without form. Therefore, whatever you see here is itself Matter," says the *rishi.*

SHLOKA 6

atha aditya udayan yat praachiim disham pravishati tena praachyaan pranaan rashmishu sannidhatte
yad dakshinaam yat pratiichiim yad udiichiim yad adho yad oordhvam yad antaraa disho yat sarvam prakaashayati
tena sarvaan pranaan rashmishu sannidhatte

"Now, the Sun, after rising, enters the Eastern side. By that he bathes with his rays all Life, in the East. When he illumines all the other sides – the South, the West, and the North, below, above and in-between – by that he bathes his rays on all living beings with Life."

That means, the *praana*, or Life Energy, in the form of the light of the Sun, bathes the entire universe, in all directions, with Life.

SHLOKA 7

sa esha vaishvaanaro vishva roopah praano agnir udayate
tad etad richa abhyuktam

"It is he, the Vaishvaanara – the Fire – assuming every form of life as Fire, who rises every day. This is declared in the verses of the Rig."

Vaishvaanara is the Fire, the Life, which is the essence of all living beings. The Life, the *praana*, the energy that glows in all human beings, is that Vaishvaanara, the essence of the whole universe. So the *rishi* says that this light, which appears as the Sun is the Vaishvaanara, the Fire that assumes every form and rises every day.

And this is what the verse in the Rig Veda also says. About the Vaishvaanara, or the Supreme Essence that pervades everything, the Upanishad declares this:

SHLOKA 8

vishva roopam harinam jaata vedasam paraayanam
jyotir ekam tapantam
sahasra rashmih shatadhaa vartamaanah praanah
prajaanaam udayaty esha sooryah

"This Vaishvaanara, this Lord who has all forms – the golden one, the Sun, the all-knowing, the goal of all, the sole light, the giver of heat; possessing thousands of rays, existing in hundreds of forms – thus rises as the Sun, the Life of all creation."

Here, the Sun is a symbol of the supreme, primordial, Life Energy; the Vaishvaanara, the Fire of Life which pervades all objects, protects all objects and gives life to everything on Earth.

The *rishi*, who is also known as the *kavi*, the poet, praises that Supreme Being in beautiful verses. "That Surya, the Life of all creation, the golden one, the all-knowing, the goal of all, the sole light, the giver of heat, possessing a thousand rays, exists in hundreds of forms." That means, there is one Reality, the essence of the Supreme that exists in hundreds of forms. As the Ishavasya Upanishad says, *Isha vasya idam sarvam* – "That Supreme Being pervades everything here."

In the next part of the Prashna Upanishad, the Year is identified with the Lord of Creation. The Upanishads and the Vedas deal with the universals and link them with the particulars, which are larger than life. "Year" or *samvat* is an abstract concept for three hundred and sixty five days. "Year after year", "hundreds of years"... "Year" is an expression and *samvatsara* means "a period of time". So here, the *rishi* says, "That period of time by which you live, grow and die, is none other than the Lord of Creation." This is the link.

SHLOKA 9

samvatsaro vai prajaapatih tasyaayane dakshinam cha uttaram cha
tad ye ha vai tad ishtaa poorte kritam ity upaasate
te chaandramasam eva lokam abhijayante, ta eva punar aavartante,
tasmaad ete rishayah prajaa kaamaa dakshinam pratipadyante
esha ha vai rayir yah pitriyaanah

"The Year verily is the Lord of creation. Of it, there are two paths – the Southern and the Northern. Now those, verily, who worship by performing sacrifice and doing pious acts, thinking these as valuable work, they devoutly live in the human world. They will certainly return again, after attaining the world of the Moon. Therefore, those sages, who desire offspring, take this Southern route – this is the path of the ancestors, the path of Matter."

Having said that the Year is the Lord of creation, the *rishi* says, in a very poetic expression, that as there are only two parts of the Year, so there are two paths – Northern and Southern, which means the upward and the downward paths. One moves either up, on the Northern Path, or down, on the Southern Path.

Those *rishis* who worship by performing sacrifice and doing pious acts, who do charity, who sacrifice themselves for others, thinking that this is the work one should do – they win the human world. But, they are not free of desire and therefore, they return again to this world, after attaining the world of the Moon. They are reborn, their life cycle is not ended, they come again – they do not move towards absolute freedom.

These sages, who are desirous of offspring, who want their glory to continue on this earth, even after they are gone, take the Southern route, because their aim is to be happy in this world and they want to leave their offspring happy in this world, after they are gone. This is the path that most ancestors have followed – this is the path of material well-being, this is the path of coming again and again to this world.

There is another path, the Northern path, which is the upward one. In *yogic* terms, the description of the movement of aspiration, thought, concentration and energy, is either upwards, towards the higher side, or downwards, towards the lower side. Moving up and down the spine is *mukhyaprana* – the Supreme Energy. When it goes down, it leads to material well-being; when it goes up, it leads to spiritual well-being. I am deliberately not using the word, *kundalini,* as it can be misunderstood. It is the ascent and descent of consciousness in two different spheres – material or spiritual.

Now the *rishi* says of those who take the Northern route, who move upwards:

SHLOKA 10

atha uttarena tapasaa brahmacharyena shraddhayaa vidyaya
atmaanam anvishya adityam abhijayante
etad vai praanaanaam aayatanam, etad amritam abhayam, etat
paraayanam, etasmaan na punar aavartante ity esha nirodhah
tad esha shlokah

"Those who seek the Self through austerity, chastity, faith and knowledge, they move by the Northern route and gain the domain of the Sun, who shines in the upper-most reaches. That is the support of all breaths, the Life Breath. When one has reached that, the Sun, which is the eternal and fearless abode, one has reached the end. About that, there is this verse."

The Life Breath, the *mukhyaprana,* the Supreme *praana,* supports all other *praanas* or movement of breath in the body. When one has reached That, at the end of the Northern path, one has reached the final goal, the Sun – the spiritual Sun. That is the eternal and fearless abode, from where one does not have to come back into this world of sorrow. That is the stopping of conditioning.

Those who have reached the Supreme Abode, the Supreme Being, the true Self, from which one does not become conditioned to be reborn again, remain eternally free and unconditioned. Such people are not reborn, for that is the final goal – they do not return.

About that Supreme Being, there is this verse, where He is spoken of as the "Father":

SHLOKA 11

pancha paadam pitaram dvadasha akritim diva aahuh pare ardhe purishinam
atheme anya u pare vichakshanam sapta chakre shadara aahur arpitam

"Some say that That Being, the Father, having five feet and twelve forms, is seated in the higher half of the heavens, full of water; and others speak of Him as the Omniscient, seated on a chariot with seven wheels and six spokes."

This means that those who follow the upward, evolutionary path, or the Northern path, as it is called, who seek the Self through austerity, chastity, faith and knowledge, gain the ultimate and reach That Supreme abode, the world of the Sun, who is called the Father. He has five feet and twelve forms, meaning the seasons and months. He is seated in the higher part of the heavens, full of water.

"Seven wheels and six spokes," indicates the psychic system of the *naadis,* which exist in the human body, and the upward movement of Energy, the *praana,* through the central channel, the *sushumnanaadi.* It refers to the Northern or the upward movement of Energy, which goes through the seven wheels, which are the seven *chakras,* which are the seven psychic centres along the *sushumna naadi* – until it reaches the highest heaven, which is the *sahasraarachakra,* full of water. Water here means the *apastattva,* or the element of liquidity, of movement, identified with the Moon or the *soma.* Having reached there, the *rishi* is never reborn, and he lives identified with the Omniscient.

Again, the *rishi* uses the symbol of Month to explain creation. He says:

SHLOKA 12

maaso vai prajaapatih tasya krishnapaksha eva rayih shuklah praanah
tasmaad eta rishayah sukhlah ishtim kurvanti itara itarasmin

"The Month verily is the Lord of creation. The dark half of the Month is Matter, or *rayih,* and the bright half of the Month is Life, or *praana.* In the bright half of the Month, some seers, the *rishis,* perform their sacrifices, while others use the other half of the month."

Those *rishis,* who seek spiritual splendour or fulfilment, and eternal freedom, use the brighter half of the Month and perform their sacrifices. And those who look for Matter, for material fulfilment, utilise the dark half of the Month and perform their sacrifices.

The idea is that there are two halves, meaning opposites – light and darkness. One moves towards the light and abjures darkness. All other symbols are used to bring this fact out clearly.

Continuing to depict duality and its opposites in creation as coming from and existing in the Supreme Unity, the Upanishad continues:

SHLOKA 13

aho raatro vai prajaapatih tasya ahar eva praano
raatrir eva rayih
praanam vaa ete praskandanti ye divaa ratyaa samyujyam te
brahmacharyam eva tad yad raatrau ratyaa samyujyante

"Day and Night are verily the Lord of creation. Day indeed is Life and Night is Matter. Those who join, who have sexual intercourse by day, dissipate their Life and those who have intercourse by night are chaste indeed."

Now this is interesting – *brahmacharya,* at least from this verse, appears to be not "complete abstinence from sex, but control of sex because the Prashna Upanishad declares, "those who have sexual intercourse by day, dissipate their life. Those who have sexual intercourse by night are chaste indeed." That means, there has to be a certain "control" of energies, not complete abstinence. The Upanishads, with all their exultation of celibacy, recognise the value of married life. Most of the *rishis* were married men.

Now, from there, the Upanishad proceeds, saying:

SHLOKA 14

annam vai prajaapatih tato ha vaitad retah tasmaad imaah
prajaah prajaayante

"Food also, indeed, is the Lord of creation, because from food comes the seed. From this, creatures here are born."

From food comes the vital material required for reproduction. From that, creatures are born.

This is the approach of the Upanishad. In one place it talks of the exalted, untouchable, unreachable, spiritual Being and then brings it down to the ordinary level of day to day things. While admitting that the Supreme Brahman is absolute, it also says that the Supreme Brahman, in this case, as far as existence is concerned, manifests itself as food. "Food indeed is the Lord of creation"; for, from this, verily, is semen created and from this, all creatures are born. Therefore, food is the manifestation of Brahman.

That *annam* or food is Brahman, is also mentioned in other Upanishads.

The Upanishad then says:

SHLOKA 15

tad ye ha vai tat prajaapati vratam charanti
te mithunam utpaadayante
teshaam evaisha brahma loko yeshaam tapo brahmacharyam
yeshu satyam pratishthitam

"Thus, those who practice this rule of the Lord of creation, produce couples. To them alone is the world of Brahma, in whom austerity, chastity and truth are established."

Those who understand the value of celibacy, as well as the value of creation; those who practice the rules by which they know how to control and use their energies at the proper time and in the proper direction attain Brahma's world of creation, as they are established in austerity, chastity and truth.

The Upanishad sees great beauty in the natural innocence and beauty of sexual life and parental love and links it to the deeper and higher energies of the cosmos. So, the Upanishad establishes the link – from the high to the middle and then to ordinary life, which is the practice of living – from the grand Brahman to what you should do in your day to day life to attain Brahman.

SHLOKA 16

teshaam asau virajo brahmaloko na yeshu jihmam anritam
na maayaa cheti

"To them is that stainless world of Brahman, in whom there is no crookedness, no falsehood and no trickery."

Or, the corollary to this would be that when there is crookedness, falsehood and trickery, one cannot hope to reach the pure world of the stainless Brahman. One has to become stainless first in one's living – otherwise, how can one proceed to the stainless Supreme Being?

Those who know how to control and use their energies properly, at the right time and the right moment, attain that stainless world, where there is no crookedness, falsehood or trickery. That means, if you have crookedness, falsehood or trickery, you cannot hope to reach that stainless world of the Supreme Brahman.

QUESTION TWO

Then Bhaargava of the Vidarbha country asks about the powers that support creation:

SHLOKA 1

atha hainam bhaargavo vaidarbhih papraccha
bhagavan katy eva devaah prajaam vidhaarayante
katara etat prakaashayante kah punar eshaam varishthah iti

"Bhaargava of Vidarbha asked him, 'Venerable Sir, Bhagavan, how many powers support the created world? How many illumine this and who among them is the greatest?'"

SHLOKA 2

tasmai sa hovaacha aakaasho ha vaa esha devo vayur
agnih aapah prithivi vaang manas chakshuh shrotram cha te
prakaashya abhivadanti vayam etad baanam avashtabhya
vidhaarayaamah

"To him he said, '*Akasha*, ether or space, is verily, such a power. Air, fire, water, earth, speech, mind, eye and ear too. They, having illumined their power, declare, 'We sustain and support this body.''"

As far as the human body is concerned, speech, by which one can communicate this Truth to others; the mind, without which we cannot even speculate on the Truth; the eye which sees the universe in its splendour and gravity; and the ear which hears both the auspicious and the inauspicious – these are those powers which illumine the body and sustain and support this body.

But the greatest of these powers is Life, *praana,* which is the sum total of everything. It is the Energy that animates everything. So Life, the greatest of these powers, is deified here.

And Life said to the rest of the Energies of the universe:

SHLOKA 3

taan varishthah praana uvaacha maa moham aapadyatha
aham evaitat panchadha atmaanam pravibhajya etat baanam
avashtabhya vidhaarayaami iti

"The chief *praana,* the Life Energy, said to them, 'Do not be deluded. I alone, dividing myself five-fold, sustain and support this body.'

The chief Life Energy divides itself into the five forms of vital breath – *prana, apana, vyana, udana, samana* – in the body, and sustains and supports it. It also divides itself into the five forms of energy – space, wind, fire, water, earth – in the universe. The one *praana* acts through the body and the universe- they are linked together.

But the mind, the eye, the ear, the speech, they did not believe him – they did not believe the deity, Life. Then they saw that he, *praana,* seemed to go upward, from the body.

SHLOKA 4

te ashraddadhaana babhoovuh
sa abhimaanaad oordhvam utkramata iva
tasminn utkraamaty yatha itare sarva eva utkraamante
tasmin cha pratishthamaane sarva eva praatishthante
tad yathaa makshikaa madhu kara raajaanam utkraamantam

sarva eva utkraamante
tasmin cha pratishtamaane sarva eva praatishthante
evam vaang manas chakshuh shrotram cha
te priitaah praanam stunvanti

"They believed him not. Out of indignation, he, *praana,* the Life Energy, the breath, seemed to go upward. When the breath went up, all other senses went up with it. When it settled down, all others settled down. Just as the bees go out when the queen bee goes out and they settle down when she settles down, even so do speech, mind, sight and hearing- they go where the Life Energy leads them. They, being satisfied, praise Life – *praana.*"

Here is a beautiful link between the universal and the particular. Just as *praana,* the Life Energy, sustains the entire universe, it also sustains the body. The Life Energy in human, which resides in the body, is the *praana*. This *pranic* Life Energy, the one vital breath, divides itself into five parts – *praana, apana, udana, samana* and *vyana* – and these sustain the functions of the body.

It is this one Energy, which moves through the central channel, or the *sushumna naadi,* when the breath is made to go up, through meditation. When the breath goes up, then the hearing, sight, feeling, mind – everything goes up with it. When it settles down, in the highest of spiritual spheres, everything settles down and there is utter peace, and there is the utter satisfaction of blissfulness, then, one praises Life. This is that one Energy, the Supreme Energy, which is the Life Energy in material things, as well as the vital breath in the human body.

SHLOKA 5

esho agnih tapaty esha soorya esha parjanyo maghavaan esha vaayuh
esha prithivii rayir devah sat asat cha amritam cha yat

"It is this Supreme Energy that, as fire, burns, as the Sun, gives light. He is that Energy, who is also the Rain God, the Wind, the Earth, the Matter. He is Being and Non-being and is immortal."

That means, this Supreme Energy is consciousness, as well as that which is unconscious and inanimate. It is also that which is immortal.

SHLOKA 6

araa iva ratha naabhau praane sarvam pratishthitam
rikho yajoomshi saamaani yajnaah kshatram brahma cha

"As spokes in the centre of a wheel, everything is established in Life – the Rig, the Yajur, the Sama, the sacrifice, the valour and the wisdom."

The Supreme Being, the Life, is the centre of the wheel, while the verses of the Rig Veda, the formulae of the Yajur Veda, the chants of the Sama Veda; and the Vedic sacrifice, the valour and the wisdom, are all spokes from the centre of the wheel. While the centre is the Supreme Being, the Life, and everything, is established in it.

SHLOKA 7

prajaapatis charasi garbhe tvam eva pratijaayase
tubhyam praana prajaastv imaa balim haranti yah
praanaih pratitishthasi

"As the Lord of the creatures, Life, you move in the womb and then are born again as a living being. O Life, creatures here bring offerings to thee, who dwells with the vital breath."

That Prajapati becomes the seed and from the father, through the mother, becomes the child. And yet, even in the child dwells that Supreme Being in the form of the vital breath.

So, can we say that the vital breath, which moves in the human body, is the final vital link to the Supreme Breath that moves in the universe? Can we ask that question?

SHLOKA 8

devaanaam asi vahnitamah pitrinaam prathamaa svadhaa
rishii naam charitam satyam atharvaangirasaam asi

"Thou, O Supreme Being, are the chief bearer of the offerings to the Gods; you are the first offering to the forefathers, the ancestors. You are that which the great *rishis* – the descendants of Atharvana and Angirasa – practice."

SHLOKA 9

indras tvam praana tejasaa rudro asi parirakshitaa
tvam antarikshe charasi sooryas tvam jyotishaam patih

"O Life; as Indra, you are the Lord of the senses. As Rudra, you are the protector. You move in the atmosphere as the Sun, the Lord of Lights."

SHLOKA 10

yadaa tvam abhivarshasy atha imaah praana
te prajaah
aanadaroopaas tishthanti kaamaaya annam
bhavishyati iti

"O Life, when you pour down rain, then these creatures breathe and live in a state of bliss, thinking that there will be food according to their desire."

SHLOKA 11

vraatyas tvam praana ekarshir attaa vishvasya satpatih
vayam aadhyasya daataarah pitaa tvam maatarishva nah

"You are ever pure, O Life, the one fire, the eater, the true Lord of all. We are the givers of what is to be eaten. O all-pervading air, Breath, you are our father."

SHLOKA 12

yaa te tanoor vaachi pratishthitaa yaa shrotre yaa cha chakshushi
yaa cha manasi santataa shivaam taam kuru ma utkramiih

"That form of yours, well-established in speech, in the ear and in the eye; which exists continuously in the mind, make that auspicious, do not get away."

Having described the Supreme Being, the Supreme Light, which is the basis of everything, the *rishi* prays and says, "That form of yours, which can be expressed by speech, which is heard in the ear and seen by the eye" – which is the Supreme Being in the form of the world; and the Supreme Being within, "which exists continuously in the mind", which gives the mind the capacity to think, which is the Consciousness, the Witness of all that happens – "make that auspicious for us. Do not go away."

SHLOKA 13

praanasya idam vashe sarvam tridive yat pratishthitam
maata iva putraan rakshasva shrish cha prajnaam cha
vidhehi nah iti

"All this is under the control of you, O Supreme Life, which is well-established in the three worlds. Protect us as a mother protects her children. Grant us prosperity and wisdom."

There is a beautiful prayer in the Devi Bhagavatam, where the devotee prays, "O noble Goddess! May this relationship of mother and child prevail unbroken between you and me, now and forever more" – *devi ho yat vyapti sadeyho janani sadeyho*

QUESTION THREE

SHLOKA 1

atha hainam kausalyas cha ashvalaayanah papraccha
bhagavan, kuta esha praano jaayate, katham aayaaty
asmin sharire, aatmaanam vaa pravibhajya katham
pratishthate, kenotkraamate, katham baahyam abhidhatte,
katham adhyaatmam iti

"Then Kausalya, the son of Ashvala, asked him, 'Venerable Sir, Bhagavan, whence is this Life, *praana,* born? How does it come into this body? How does it distribute itself and establish itself? In what way does it depart? How does it support what is external? How does it support what relates to the individual Self? Please explain this to me."

Pippalada was well pleased.

SHLOKA 2

tasmai sa hovaacha ati prashnaan pricchasi brahmishtha asi iti
tasmad te ham te braviimi

"To him (Kausalya) he said, 'You are asking questions which are highly transcendental. Because I think you are most devoted to Brahman, the Supreme Being, and therefore I will tell you.'"

SHLOKA 3

aatmanaa esha praano jaayate
yatha esha purushe chaya etasminn etad aatatam manokrutena
ayaati asminn shariire

"This Life, *praana,* is born of the Self. As in the case of a person, there is this shadow, so is this Life connected with the Self. It comes into this body with the activity of the mind."

"This Life is born of the Self" – "Self", meaning the inner Self, the *atman,* not the body. With the activity of the mind, with the activity of thought, Life comes into this body. The *rishi* gives an interesting example. He says that just as a person has a shadow and the shadow looks in many ways, similarly the body is only a shadow. Although the body looks like the Self, it is the shadow of the true Self, which is the *atman.*

How does Life come into the body? It is in the body because of the activity of thought. When thought ceases, it does not act in the body. It is free, it is back to its original state. When thought functions, the shadow is mistaken for the Reality.

The *rishi* gives another example:

SHLOKA 4

yathaa samraat eva adhikritaan viniyunkte
etaan graamaan etaan graamaan adhitishthasva iti
evam eva esha praanah itaraan praanaan prithak
prithag eva sannidhatte

"As a sovereign commands his officers, saying 'You superintend such and such village,' even so does this Life allot the other vital breaths to their respective places."

This *praana,* this *mukhya praana,* this Supreme Energy allots the various functions to the other vital breaths, in their respective places, just as a king commands his officers – "You do this, you do that."

The *rishi* tells about the different breaths that come from the one Breath, the Life, *praana*:

SHLOKA 5

paayu upaasthe apaanam
chakshuh shrotre mukha naasikaabyaam praanah
svayam pratishtate
madhye tu samaanah
esha hy etadd hutam annam samam nayati
tasmaad etaah saptaarchisho bhavanti

"The out-breath, the *apaana,* is in the organs of excretion and regeneration. The Life Breath, *praana,* himself, is in the eye and the ear, and also in the mouth and the nose. In the middle is the equalizing breath, *samaana.* It is this that equalises whatever is offered as food. From it arise the seven flames."

Here, a distinction, or differentiation, is made between the different breaths, which come from the one Breath, *praana,* the Energy of Breath, or the Energy of Life. This one Breath, the *praana,* is divided into five breaths – the out-breath *apaana,* the equalizing-breath *samaana,* the life-breath *praana,* the up-breath *udaana* and the diffused-breath *vyaana.* Their function is to maintain the body.

It means that breath, which is the out-breath, the *apaana,* operates the excretion and regeneration.

The Life Breath, which is the *praana,* is in the eye, the ear, the mouth and the nose. It is that which makes us speak, it is that which makes us hear and it is that which makes us see.

In the middle is the equalising breath, the *samaana.* It is this that equalises whatever is offered as food. That means it equalises all these breaths and it also digests the food – combustion is required to digest food.

From this breath arise "the seven flames". Now, wherever you find mention of "seven flames" or "seven wheels", you can be sure it refers to the psychic apparatus or the *chakra* system, in the human body. So the "seven flames" are the Energies that are active in the centres of psychic perception.

Continuing, the *rishi* says:

SHLOKA 6

hrudy hy esha aatmaa atra etad ekashatam naadiinaam
taasaam shatam shatam ekaikasyaam dvaasaptatir dvaasaptatih
pratishaakhaa naadii sahasraani bhavanti
aasu vyaanas charati

"The Supreme Self is in the heart. Here, there are a hundred and one arteries. To each one of these belong a hundred smaller arteries. To each of these belong seventy two thousand branching arteries. Within them moves the diffused breath, *vyaana.*"

SHLOKA 7

atha ekaya urdhva udaanah punyena punya lokam nayati
paapena paapam ubhaabhyaam eva manushya lokam

"Now, rising upwards, through one of these, the up-breath, the *udaana,* leads the soul, in consequence of the good work, to the good world and in consequence of the evil, to the evil world; and, in consequence of both, to the world of men."

Wherever this breath is diverted, up or down, higher or lower, decides the fate of the human being.

Then the *rishi* connects the Breath in the human body with that which is the eternal Energy of the visible universe:

SHLOKA 8

adityo ha vai baahyah praana udayati esha hy enam
chakshusham praanam anugrahnaanah
prithivyaam yaa devataa sa eshaa
purushasya apaanam avashtabhya
antaraa yad akaashah sa samaano vaayur vyaanah

"The sun verily rises as the external Life, for it is that which helps the Life-Breath, the *praana,* in the eye. The divinity, which is in the earth, supports a person's out-breath, the *apaana.* What is between the sun and the earth is the equalising breath, the *samaana.* Air is the diffused breath, *vyaana.*"

The sun rises as the external Life, *praana,* and it helps the *praana* in the eye – for, without light, one cannot see. The earth supports a person's out-breath, *apaana.* The space is the equalising-breath, *samaana.* The air is the diffused-breath, *vyaana,* which is available for all creatures to breathe and be sustained.

SHLOKA 9

tejo ha vai udaanah
tasmaat upashaanta tejaah punarbhavam
indriyair manasi sampadyamaanaih

"Fire is verily the up-breath, *udaana.* Therefore, he whose fire of Life has ceased goes to rebirth with his senses sunk in the mind."

He who thus leaves the body, in whom the fire of Life is moving upwards, in whom the aspiration for freedom is gone, comes back to earth because his sensory perceptions, his desires are still sunk in the mind. Therefore, he goes to rebirth.

SHLOKA 10

yat chittas tena esha praanam aayaati
praanas tejasaa yuktah
saha atmanaa yathaa samkalpitam lokam nayati

"Whatever is one's thinking, therewith one enters into Life, *praana.* His Life, combined with fire, along with the Self, leads to whatever world has been fashioned by thought."

The Upanishad hits upon the most important aspect of all thinking, which is, whatever you think you want to be, that you become. Whatever one is thinking of at the time of death, one enters into Life, in that form. The fire of desire catches on to that which you want to become, and the Self leads you to whatever world has been fashioned by you in thought, as desired by you and you attain that. If you are caught by this world, you will naturally come back to this world.

The *rishi* then tells about what happens to the wise man who understands Life, *praana,* in all its aspects:

SHLOKA 7

ya evam vidvaan praanam veda
na haasya prajaa hiiyate amrito bhavati
tad esha shlokah

"The wise one who knows Life thus, to him there shall be no continuation. He becomes immortal. As to this, there is this verse:"

"Off-spring" is the word used, but it means "continuation". The wise man who understands Life, *praana,* will have no continuation of the cycle of birth and death. He is free from rebirth as he becomes immortal.

As to this, there is the following verse:

SHLOKA 12

utpattim aayatim sthaanam vibhutvam cha eva panchadhaa
adhyaatmam cha eva praanasya vijnaaya amritam ashnute
vijnaayam amritam ashnuta iti

"The birth of Life, *praana* – its entry, its abode, its five-fold overlordship and its relationship to the Self; knowing these, one attains immortality, knowing these, one attains immortality."

The wise man who understands Life, *praana,* in all its aspects – its origin, its abode, its five-fold division and its relationship to the Self attains immortality. Knowing that your mind takes you to where you want to go, and what you think you attain, the wise one attains immortality.

So far, three questions have been answered. There are three more questions to answer, in this Upanishad.

QUESTION FOUR

Gargya, the grandson of Surya, asked the *rishi* Pippalada, the next question about the waking, dream and deep sleep states:

SHLOKA 1

atha hainam sauryaayanii gaargyah papraccha
bhagavan etasmin purushe kaani svapanti kaany asmin jaagrati
katara esha devah svapnaan pashyati kasya etat sukham bhavati
kasmin nu sarve sampratishthita bhavanti iti

"Then Gargya, the grandson of Surya, asked him, 'Reverend Sir, what are they that sleep in a person? What are they that keep awake in him? What is the God that sees dreams? Whose is this happiness? In whom are all these established?"

Where do all these mystifying things come from? What happens when we sleep? Everybody sleeps – the hard-working labourer or the chief of a company, everyone goes to sleep. And when they sleep, neither is aware of one's own existence. When they wake up, they are back again to their own, usual daily cycle. So what happens when one sleeps? What happens when one wakes up? How are they linked together?

Pippalada then said to him:

SHLOKA 2

tasmai sa hovaacha: yathaa gaargya marichayah arkasya astam
gacchatah sarvaa etasmin tejo mandala ekii bhavanti
taah punah punar udayatah pracharanti
evam ha vai tat sarvam pare deve manasy ekii bhavati
tena tarhy esha purusho na shrunoti na pashyati na jighrati
na rasayate na sprushate na abhivadate na aadatte na aanandayate
na visrujate na iyaayate svapiti iti aachakshate

"He said to him, 'O Gargya! As all the rays of the setting sun become one in the circle of light, and as they spread forth again when he rises again, even so does all this become one in the superior god, which is the mind. Hence the person hears not, sees not, smells not, tastes not, touches not, speaks not, takes not, rejoices not, emits not and moves not. Then, they say, 'He sleeps.''"

When everything has ceased, when all the sensations have ceased and withdrawn, like the rays of the sun to the centre of the sun, in that state, the *rishi* says, when one falls asleep, everything goes back to the centre, which is the Superior God, the Mind.

About two thousand years ago, at a conservative estimate, much before the modern psychologist, the *rishi* says – that everything is in the mind. Everything starts with the mind. He calls the mind "the superior god" where everything converges when we sleep, like the rays of the setting sun and from where everything starts again like the rising sun, when we wake up.

In sleep, though the senses are dormant, the Life Energy, *praana*, remains active. Here, the different parts of the Life Energy are used for different oblations and Life is conceived of as a sacrifice, *yagnya*:

SHLOKA 3

praana agnaya eva etasmin pure jaagrati
gaarhapatyo ha vaa esha apaanah vyaanah anvaahaarya pachanah
yad gaarhapatyaat praniiyate praanayanaad aahavaniiyah praanah

"The fires of Life, *praana*, alone remain awake in the city – the body. The householder's fire is the out-breath; the southern sacrificial fire is the diffused breath; and the oblation fire is the in-breath, since it is taken from the householder's fire."

Here, Life is conceived of as a sacrifice, and the three breaths are symbolically identified with the fires used in the Vedic sacrifice:

The *garhapatya* is the householder's fire, which is the sacred fire that is kept burning in all homes and all other fires are taken from it.

The householder's fire is the out-breath – *apaana.*

The southern sacrificial fire, *anvaahaaryapachana,* is that fire into which oblations to the forefathers are offered. It is the diffused breath – *vyaana.*

The oblation fire, *ahavaniya,* is that fire into which oblations to the gods are offered. It is the in-breath – *praana.*

To keep the body alive, the different parts of the Life Energy remain functioning; the out-breath, the in-breath and that which is between the inner and the outer breath, the equalizing breath – the *samaana.*

SHLOKA 4

yad ucchvaasa nihshvaasaav etaav aahutii samam nayati
iti samaanah
mano ha vaa va yajamaanah ishta phalam eva udaanah
sa evam yajamaanam ahar ahar brahma gamayati

"As the equalising breath, *samaana* carries equally the in-breath and the out-breath as the oblations; so *samaana* is the priest. The mind is the one who performs the sacrifice, the *yajamaanah*, the sacrificer. The fruit of the sacrifice is the up-breath, *udaana*; it leads the sacrificer everyday to Brahman."

The up-breath, *udaana*, takes the mind, the sacrificer, everyday to Brahman, in deep sleep. But the one who practices *yoga* will understand what the word, "up-breath" means. When the mind and the *praana* are completely moving upwards, which means moving to the higher states of consciousness, then, one is daily, constantly in touch with the highest Supreme Reality, which is the super-conscious state.

SHLOKA 5

atra esha devah svapne mahimaanam anubhavati
yad drushtam drushtam anupashyati
shrutam shrutam eva artham anushrunoti
desha digantaraish cha praty anubhootam
punah punah praty anubhavati drushtam cha adrushtam cha
shrutam cha ashrutam cha anubhootam cha ananubhootam cha
sat cha asat cha sarvam pashyati sarvah pashyati

"There in that sleep, that god (meaning the mind) experiences greatness. He sees again what object has been seen; he hears again whatever has been heard; he experiences again and again whatever has been experienced in different places and directions. He sees what has been seen and also what has not been seen; what has been heard and what has not been heard; what has been experienced and what has not been experienced; what is existent and what is not existent. He sees all."

The mind at rest, free from the trammels, the conditionings of sensory data, becomes once again, all-powerful and all-pervading and sees everything and experiences everything, because, says the *rishi*, "He is all." Being all, he sees all.

What happens then?

SHLOKA 6

sa yaada tejasa abhibhooto bhavati
atra esha devah svapnaan na pashyati
atha tad etasmin shariire etat sukham bhavati

"When he (the mind) is overcome with light, that god sees no dreams. Then, here, in this body, arises great happiness."

When the consciousness is moved to the highest realm, with the up-breath; when the mind has become quiet, absolutely still, at rest, tranquil, peaceful and auspicious, then that mind is filled with light. In such a state, that mind sees no dreams. Then here, in this body, arises the great happiness of dreamless sleep, *sushupti*.

SHLOKA 7

sa yathaa saumya vayaamsi vaaso vruksham sampratishthante
evam ha vai tat sarvam para aatmani sampratishthante

"Even as birds, O dear one, resort to a tree for a resting place, so does everything here resorts to the Supreme Self and finds its rest."

So, every night, after all the activity, action and exhaustion, when the mind goes back to sleep, filled with light, it sees no dreams and is happy. Even as birds perch and rest in a tree, so does the mind rest in the Supreme Self, because the Supreme Self is the all-restful Being.

What finds rest in the Supreme Self? The *rishi* says:

SHLOKA 8

prithivii cha prithivii maatraa cha aapas cha aapomaatraa cha
tejas cha tejomaatraa cha vayus cha vaayumaatraa cha
aakaashas cha aakaashamaatraa cha chakshus cha
drashtavyam cha shrotram cha shrotavyam cha

ghraanam cha ghraatavyam cha
rasas cha rasayitavyam cha tvak cha sparshayitavyam cha
vaak cha vaktavyam cha hastau cha adaatavyam cha
upasthas cha anandayitavyam cha paayus cha visarjayitavyam cha
paadau cha gantavyam cha manas cha mantavyam cha
buddhis cha boddhavyam cha ahamkaaras cha ahamkartavyam cha
chittam cha chetayitavyam cha tejas cha vidyotayitavyam cha
praanas cha viddhaarayitavyam cha

"The earth and the elements of earth; water and the elements of water; fire and the elements of fire; air and the elements of air; ether and the elements of ether; sight and what can be seen; hearing and what can be heard; smell and what can be smelled; taste and what can be tasted; the skin and what can be touched; the organ of speech and what can be spoken; hands and what can be handled; the organ of generation and what can be enjoyed; the organ of excretion and what can be excreted; the feet and what can be walked to; the mind and what can be perceived; the intellect and what can be conceived; the self-sense and what can be connected with the self; thought and what can be thought; radiance and what can be illumined and the Life-Breath and what can be supported by it – all these rest in the Self, the *atman*, in sleep."

SHLOKA 9

esha hi drashtaa sprashtaa shrotaa ghraataa rasayitaa
mantaa boddhaa kartaa vijnaanaatmaa purushah sa pare
akshara aatmani sampratishthate

"He, the Person, verily is the seer, the toucher, the hearer, the smeller, the taster, the perceiver, the knower, the doer, the thinking Self. He becomes established in the Supreme, undecaying Self."

It means that the subject Self, which is the Awareness of all that is going on, which enjoys itself in deep sleep, which also enjoys dreams and can also be beyond that position and be established in its own state – that state, which is in the spirit, transcends duality of subject and object. In that, he remains in the Supreme, undecaying Self.

SHLOKA 10

param eva aksharam pratipadyate sa yo ha vai tad acchaayam
ashariiram alohitam shubhram aksharam vedayate
yas tu saumya sa sarvajnaah sarvo bhavati tad esha shlokah

"Therefore he, who knows the shadowless, bodiless, colourless, pure, undecaying Self, attains verily the Supreme, undecaying Self. He who, O dear one, knows this, becomes omniscient; he becomes all. As to this, there is this verse:"

SHLOKA 11

vijnaanaatmaa saha devaish cha sarvaih
praanaa bhootaani sampratishthanti yatra
tad aksharam vedayate yas tu saumya
sa sarvajnah sarvam eva avivesha iti

"He who knows that undecaying Self, which is of the nature of intelligence, in which is established the vital breath, *praana,* and the elements along with all the gods, the senses, becomes omniscient and enters all."

QUESTION FIVE

SHLOKA 1

atha ha enam shaibyas satyakaamah papraccha
sa yo ha vai tad bhagavan manushyeshu
praayanaantam aumkaaram abhidhyaayiita
katamam vaa va sa tena lokam jayati iti

"Then Satyakaama, the son of Shibi, asked him, 'Venerable Sir, by doing this, what world does he win, who, among men, meditates on that *aumkaara,* until the end of his life?'

Although Satyakaama here has been depicted as the son of Shibi, he represents anyone who wants to know the Truth, who is not interested in anything else.

Satyakaama wanted to know what happens to people who chant *aum* and meditate on the syllable *aum,* until the end of their lives. He asked the *rishi* Pippalada, the most important question: What world do such people attain, by meditating on *aum*? Where do they go? What do they get?

Pippalada said to him:

SHLOKA 2

tasmai sa ha uvaacha
etad vai satyakaama param cha aparam cha brahma
yad aumkaarah
tasmaad vidvaan etenaivaayatanena ekataram anveti

"That which is the sound *aum,* O Satyakaama, is both the higher and the lower Brahman. Therefore, with this support alone, does the wise man reach the one or the other."

Now, "the higher and the lower Brahman" needs to be explained. "The lower Brahman" means the qualified, personal Ishwara, or the Supreme Energy, or the Supreme Brahman conceived as the Creator, the Preserver and the Destroyer, who can be worshipped and so on. "The higher Brahman" is the highest, the absolute Brahman, which is the unqualified, absolute Self, which cannot be defined or held in our mind.

So what Pippalada meant was that the sound *aum* is the most important support for the wise to reach, either the personal Ishwara, or the unqualified, absolute Brahman.

The *rishi* gives details about what happens when a person meditates on the elements or syllables of *aum* – *"a", "u" and "m"*:

SHLOKA 3

sa yady eka maatram abhidhyaayiita
sa tena eva samveditas toornam eva jagatyaam abhisampadyate
tam richo manushya lokam upanayante sa tatra
tapaasa brahmacharyena shraddhayaa sampanno
mahimaanam anubhavati

"If he meditates on the first element, '*a*', he is enlightened by that. He comes back quickly to this world, after death. The verses of the Rig Veda lead him to the world of men. There, endowed with austerity, chastity and faith, he experiences greatness."

"*a*" is the first syllable in the sound *aum.* It is the beginning of everything: "*a*" – *akshara* or "indestructible". It is the beginning of all sounds which even the dumb can pronounce.

If a person meditates on "*a*", the first syllable of *aum,* and contemplates on it–on the sound as well as the meaning of it–he becomes enlightened enough to come back quickly to the world of men, after death. And there, not as an ordinary person, but as one endowed with austerity, chastity and faith. There he attains greatness in life. This is the result of meditating on the first syllable "*a*".

I am translating *shraddha* as "faith". It also means "one-pointedness, complete attention and the eagerness to find the Truth." So it is faith in one's Self, in one's capacity to find the Truth that leads one to greatness.

What happens to a person when he meditates on the second syllable "*u*", or the two elements, "*au*" of "*aum*"? The *rishi* continues:

SHLOKA 4

atha yadi dvi maatrena manasi sampadyate
sa antariksham yajurbhir unniiyate soma lokam
sa soma loke vibhootim anubhooya punar aavartate

"Then if he meditates on the two elements, he attains the mind. He learns the formulae. The Yajur takes him to the world of the Moon in the intermediary space, after death. Having experienced greatness there, he returns again."

So, a person, who meditates on the two elements of *aum,* on "*a*" and "*u*" – "*au*" – attains the mind. He becomes an expert in being able to work on the creative aspect of his mind. After death, he is taken to the world of the Moon, where he experiences greatness. He is able to do anything that he imagines, living in the world of imagination, because, the moon is associated with imagination, visualisation, creativity of thought, which of course, when goes beyond control, becomes lunacy – the word "lunar" is related to lunacy.

So, after living in the world of visualisation, living and enjoying the world which he visualises with his imagination, he returns again to this earth, from the inter-space, to further evolve and attain greater levels of understanding.

SHLOKA 5

yah punar etam tri maatrena aum
ity etena iva aksharena param purusham abhidhyaayiita
sa tejasi soorye sampannah
yathaa paadodaras tvacha vinirmuchyata evam ha vai sa paapmanaa
vinirmuktah sa saamabhir unniiyate brahma lokam
sa etasmaat jiivaghanaat paraat param purishayam purusham
iikshate tad etau shlokau bhavatah

"Then, he who meditates on the highest Person, with the three elements of *aum*–"*a*", "*u*", "*m*"– becomes one with the highest Light, which is the Sun. As a snake is freed from its skin, even so he is freed from sins. After death, he is led by the chanting of the Saama hymns to the world of Brahma. From this highest Light, he sees the Person that dwells in the body. As to this, there are these two verses:"

SHLOKA 6

tisro maatraa mrityumatyah prayuktaa
anyonya saktaa anavi prayuktaah

kriyaasu baahyaabhyantara madhyamaasu samyak prayuktaasu
na kampate jnah

"Now, these are the three elements, each leading to death, if taken by themselves and separately practiced. But if they are connected to each other without being separated, they are well-employed in all the actions – external, internal or intermediate–and the knower does not waver (in meditation)."

A person who knows the significance of meditating on the three elements does not waver from the meditation. He moves forward.

Pippalada continues in the next verse:

SHLOKA 7

rigbhir etam yajurbhir antariksham
saamabhir yat tat kavayo vedayante
tam aumkaarena eva ayatanena anveti vidvaan
yat tat chaantam ajaram amritam abhayam param cha

"With the Rig verses, one attains this world; with the Yajur formulae, one attains the inter-space and with the Saama chants, one attains that which the *rishis* recognise. Also, even by the mere sound *aum* as the support, the wise one attains That which is tranquil, unageing, immortal, fearless and supreme."

What can a person do to attain higher levels of understanding?

With the understanding of the teachings of the Rik verses, the hymns, he can attain this world.

With the understanding of the formulae of the Yajur, by which one imagines, he can attain higher levels of understanding; he can attain the inter-space, which means, he ascends above earthly existence. With the Saama chants, the sacred hymns, which are tuned to lift one up, he can attain the highest state of consciousness, which the great *rishis* recognise. He attains that when he practices all the three together – the Rik, the Yajur and the Saama.

Now, says the Upanishad, the wise one attains that stage merely by the sound, *aum*. He does not have to go through the Rik, the Yajur and the Saama, as *aum* is the essence of the Rik, the Yajur and the Saama. And when the wise one takes refuge in the sound *aum,* as the support, then he attains that, which is by itself, tranquil, unageing, immortal, fearless and supreme. He goes beyond all the three states. That is the *tureeya,* and it underlies all other states and transcends them.

QUESTION SIX

Sukesha, son of Bhaaradvaaja, asks Pippalada about the Supreme Being, the Person of sixteen parts, the *Purusha.*

SHLOKA 1

atha ha enam sukeshaa bhaaradvaajah papraccha
bhagavan hiranyanaabhah kausalyo raaja putro maam upetya
etam prashnam apricchata shodasha kalam bhaaradvaaja purusham
vettha tam aham kumaaram abruvam
na aham imam veda yady aham imam avedisham katham te
na avakshyam iti
sa moolo vaa esha parishushyati yo anritam abhivadati
tasmaan na arhamy anritam vaktum sa tooshniim ratham
aaruhya pravavraaja
tam tvaa pricchaami kvaasau purushah iti

"Sukesha, son of Bhaaradvaaja, said to him, 'Venerable Sir, Hiranyanaabha, a prince of the Kosala kingdom, approached me, and asked this question, 'Bhaaradvaaja, do you know the Person who is of sixteen parts?'

I replied to the prince, 'I know him not. If I had known him, why should I not tell you about it? Verily, he who speaks an untruth withers to his roots. Therefore, it is not proper for me to speak untruth.' In silence, he mounted his chariot and departed.

So, I ask you Sir, where is that Person?'"

Sukesha, the son of the great *rishi* Bhaaradvaaja, told Pippalada that he was once asked by Hiranyanaabha, a prince of the Kosala kingdom, if he knew the Person who is of sixteen parts. Sukesha said to the prince, "I know him not." That was a fact.

He did not know the Person who is of sixteen parts. He did not try to hide his ignorance and say, "You are not ready for it, so I cannot tell you." He did not say, "I know, but I cannot tell you." He did not say all that because he believed in the Vedic dictum that "He who speaks an untruth, withers to his roots." This shows his great dedication to the truth. We cannot hope to find the Supreme Absolute Truth if we cannot stick to truth in day-to-day matters.

Pippalada said to him:

SHLOKA 2

tasmai sa ha uvaacha iha eva antah shariire saumya
sa purusho yasminn etaah shodasha kalaah prabhavanti iti

"He said to him, 'Even here within this body, O dear friend, is that Person or *Purusha,* in whom the sixteen parts arise.'"

In the Sankhya system of philosophy, the great *rishi* Kapila talks of "the Self of sixteen parts," and calls it the *linga sharira* or "the subtle body", and here, the same thing is referred to, with some modifications.

He reflected to himself about the Person within this body:

SHLOKA 3

sa iikshaamchakre kasminn aham utkraanta utkraanto
bhavishyaami
kasmin vaa pratishthite pratishthaasyaami iti

"He reflected, 'In whose departure shall I be departing and in whose settling down shall I be settling down (in the body)?'"

Then the *rishi* tells him how the sixteen parts of creation proceed from the Person, the *purusha*:

SHLOKA 4

sa praanam asrijata praanaat shraddhaam kham vaayur jyotir aapah prithivi indriyam manah annam annaad viiryam, tapo mantraah karma lokaah lokeshu cha naama cha

"He created life from Life, *praana.*From life came faith, ether, air, fire, water, earth, senses, mind and food. From food came vigour, austerity, the hymns, works and worlds; and in the world was created name."

"That Supreme Being of the sixteen parts" created Life, *praana* or Energy. So from Him proceeds Life; from Life came *shraddha* or one-pointedness and then *kham* or ether; then came *vaayu* or air; then *jyoti* or light, meaning fire; then *aapah* or water and *prithivi* or earth – these mean the vapour, the liquid and the solid. Then came *indriyam* or senses, the organs of perception; then *manah* or mind; and *annam* or food. From food came *viryam* or vigour, vitality, strength and energy. From energy came *tapah* or austerity, *mantrah* or the capacity to chant and *karma* or the ability to work or perform action. Then came *lokah* or worlds and in the worlds came *naama* or name.

"Name" suggests individuation. It is only by giving a name to something, a label, that one thing is distinguished from another. Everything is distinguished by their names.

So this is the description of the sixteen parts, which proceed from the Person, the *purusha,* who is seated in the body.

Next, these sixteen parts are compared to the rivers; while the Person is the ocean.

SHLOKA 5

sa yatha imaa nadyah syandamaanaah samudraayanaah samudram praapya astam gacchanti bhidyete taasaam naamaroope samudra ity evam prochyate
evam eva asya paridrashtur imah shodasha kalaah
purushaayanaah purusham praapya ashtam gacchanti
bhidyete chaasaam naama roope purusha ity evam prochyate

sa esho akala amrito bhavati
tad esha shlokah

"The flowing rivers that tend towards the ocean, disappear into it, and on reaching the ocean, their names and shapes being broken up, they lose their individualities and are simply called "ocean". Even so of the Seer, whose sixteen parts, though resting in the Person, on reaching the Person, disappear; their names and shapes broken up, they are simply called 'the Person'. That Person is One, without parts and is immortal. As to that, there is this verse."

Here, all the sixteen parts that exist are compared to the many rivers, which have their own individuality, their own names, their own shapes, their own forms. When they flow into the ocean, then they are one ocean. The sixteen parts become one ocean, which is the one Person. They disappear – their *nama-rupa,* or names and shapes, are broken up and there is only one Person, the *purusha.*

The one Person, who possessed the sixteen parts, is now back to being the one Person. "That One is without parts and immortal. As to that, there is this verse."

We find the same in the Tao teaching: "All under heavens will come as streams and torrents to flow into a great river or the sea."

Jalaluddin Rumi says, "A drop may enter the sea." In the Shams-e-Tabrez, he says, "None has knowledge of each who enters, that 'he is so and so'. All is gone and there is only the ocean."

Sri Ramakrishna Paramahamsa used to say that it is like the salt-doll trying to find the depth of the ocean. There is no salt-doll left any more – there is just the ocean.

There was this great English poet, Christina Rosetti, whose poems I was taught by a wonderful teacher, Harihara Iyer, in the Model High School, Trivandrum. His way of teaching was so good that I can never forget it. In a beautiful poem, Christina Rossetti says:

"Lord, we are rivers running to thy sea!
Our waves and ripples all derived from thee;
And nothing we should have and nothing to be – except for thee!"

The verse that follows, talks about this. The *rishi* gives another simile:

SHLOKA 6

araa iva ratha naabhau kaala yasmin pratishtitaah
tam vedyam purusham veda yathaa maa vo mrityuh parivyathaah

"In whom the parts are well-established as spokes in the centre of the wheel; know Him as the Person, worthy to be known, so that death may not afflict you."

The sixteen parts were first compared to the rivers which lose their identity in the ocean, the *purusha.* Here, the parts are compared to spokes that rest in the *purusha,* the centre of the wheel.

Then comes the conclusion of the instruction, after all the questions have been asked and discussed, and *samvaada* or dialogue has taken place.

What does the great *rishi* Pippalada say, in conclusion? He does not say, "This is the absolute Truth I have given you!" That would be arrogance.

So how does Pippalada conclude his instruction? What does he say to the students?

SHLOKA 7

taan hovaacha etaavad evaaham etat param brahma veda
na atah param asti iti

"He then said to them, 'Only thus far do I know that Supreme Brahman. There is none higher than that Supreme Being.'"

The more you know, the more remains to be known. The problem is when somebody says, "I have understood the Brahman completely," he does not know the Brahman at all. For, It is so immeasurable and infinite, that no one can claim that he knows the Brahman with his puny brain, which is only one chromosome different from that of the chimpanzee!

The students praised rishi Pippalada and said:

SHLOKA 8

te tam archayantah tvam hi nah pitaa
yah asmaakam avidyaayaah param paaram taarayasi iti
namah parama rishibhyo namah parama rishibhyah

"They worshipped, praising him, 'Thou indeed are our father, who does take us across to the other shore beyond ignorance. Salutations to the supreme *rishis*! Salutations to the supreme *rishis*!'"

Here a distinction is being made between our physical father and our teacher. Here, the *rishi* is addressed using the beautiful expression, *nah pitaa* or "our father". The teacher is the one who helps us know the Truth, so he is the "spiritual father", who is distinct from the "physical father", who has given us birth.

So, the students praised the *rishi* Pippalada. Any action performed in praise of the Supreme is *archana*. Not only a ritual, even praise, is *archana*. The students praised their teacher, "You, who have taken us across to the other shore, beyond ignorance, you are indeed our father. Salutations to the supreme *rishis*! Salutations to the supreme *rishis*!"

Here ends the Prashna Upanishad, the Upanishad of questions.

I would now like to elaborate on That Supreme Being, who has been referred to, in the Prashna Upanishad, by Pippalada, as "That Person of sixteen parts" and go into another Upanishad, the Shvetaashvataara Upanishad – "The Upanishad of the White Horse" – where there is the description of the Supreme Cosmic Person:

sarva aanana shiro griivah sarva bhoota guhaashayah
sarva vyaapii sa bhagavaan stasmaat sarvagatah shivah

"He, who is in the faces, heads and necks of all; who also dwells in the caves of all beings; who is all-pervading; He is the Lord and He is none other than the omnipresent Shiva."

Even though that Person dwells in secret, hidden in all beings – hidden in the hearts of all beings – He is all-pervading, the omnipresent Shiva. That Supreme Being, indeed, is the great Lord, the Emperor and the Highest Being. He is the Ruler, the imperishable Light.

When the Upanishad says, *bhagavaan,* it means what the Bhagavatam describes as *bhagavaan:*

aishwarasya samagrasya dharmasya yashasah shriyah jnaana vairagyayos cha eva sannaam bhaga itiiranaa

"He who has the six qualities of lordship, righteousness, fame, prosperity, wisdom and renunciation, is Bhagavaan."

Then follows another description of the Supreme Being, which connects it to oneself, to the heart of the human being, and to some abstract, indefinable, unreachable substance. What is that?

angushtah matraah purusho antaraatmaa sadaa janaanam hridaye sannivishtah hridaa manavisho manaasabhi klapto ya etad vidur amritas te bhavanti

"He is a Person of the measure of a thumb. He is the inner Self of all beings, ever dwelling in the hearts of men. He is the Lord of knowledge, framed by the heart and the mind. He who knows this becomes immortal."

Those who know that the Supreme Lord, resides in the heart in the little shape "of the measure of a thumb," become immortal. And, it is this little Person, who is in the heart, who is of just the measure of a thumb, who is also "the Person who has a thousand heads, a thousand eyes, a thousand feet; who surrounds the earth on all sides, stands ten fingers breadth beyond." How poetic is this description!

sahasra shirshaa purushah sahasraakshah sahasrapaad sabhoomim vishvato vritvaa aty atishtad

That little "spark", which is in the heart of man, of the human being, that little "spark" is the Supreme Being, ever-dwelling in the heart, knowing whom, men become immortal. This is the same one "with a thousand heads, a thousand eyes, a thousand feet." He is greater even than the earth, as he surrounds the earth on all sides and stands ten fingers breadth beyond the whole world.

purusha evedam sarvam yad bhootam yat cha bhavyam
utaamritatvasyesha ano yad annenaatirohati

"That Person is truly this whole world, meaning the whole universe, whatever has been and whatever will be. That Person is also the Lord of immortality and whatever grows by way of food."

That means, everything that grows, everything that lives, and everything that is here, there, anywhere; and whatever was and whatever will be, all that there is – everything is pervaded by that Supreme Being.

"On every side, It has a hand and a foot; and on every side, an eye, head and face. It has an ear everywhere. It stands encompassing all the worlds."

sarvatah paani paadam tat sarvato akshi shiro mukham
sarvatah shrutimal loke sarvam aavritya tishthati

"Reflecting the qualities of all these senses, and yet devoid of all the senses, that Supreme Being is the Lord and Ruler and the great Refuge of all."

Understand that Supreme Being, because of whom all the senses function, and yet He is devoid of all senses – He is the Lord and Ruler and above all, and most important of all, He is the Refuge of all.

sarvasya prabhum eshaanam sarvasya sharanam brihat

That means, finally, after going through everything, after being tossed around by the vagaries of nature and the foolishness of our own actions, one finally surrenders and finds supreme rest in the great Refuge, in that Supreme, all-pervading Being, who need not be searched for anywhere as He resides in the deep recesses of one's own heart. What a wonderful message!

Can we think about it for a second? Isn't it profound and moving? Isn't it a way out of the confusion and the conflict and the pain and the sorrow?

"The embodied soul, in the city of nine gates, sports, moving to and fro in the outside world, yet is the controller of the whole world – the stationary and the moving."

nava dvaare pure dehii hamso leelayate bahih
vasi sarvasya lokasya sthaavarasya charasya cha

So, this embodied soul, this "thumb-sized Being", sits in "the city of nine gates", which is the human body, moving to and fro, sporting in the outside world. Yet, He is the controller of the whole world – the world that moves and the world that does not.

"Without foot or hand, yet swift and grasping; that Being sees without eyes, and hears without ears and knows whatever is to be known; although of Him, there is none who knows."

They call that Being the Primeval Being, the Supreme Person. That Supreme Person has "no foot or hand", yet, He is so swift that He can grasp faster than anything. He sees without eyes; without ears, He hears; He knows whatever is to be known; of Him, there is none who knows.

sa vetti vedyam na cha tasyaati vettaa tam aahur agryam
purusham mahaantam

That Supreme Person is again described as, "Subtler than the subtle; greater than the great is that Self. Seated in the cave of the heart of the creature, one beholds Him as being action-less and becomes free from sorrow, when, through the grace of the Creator, he sees the Lord and His majesty."

anor anaiyaa mahato mahiiyan aatmaa guhaayaan nihito asya jantoh
tam akratum pashyati veeta shoko dhaatuh prasaadaan mahimaanam eshaam

When that Supreme Being is seen, then one is freed and becomes free from action and sorrow, through the grace of that Supreme Creator, who Himself is that Supreme Self. He sees the Lord and His majesty.

Then the *rishi* says, "I know that undecaying, ancient, primeval Self of all, present in everything on account of infinity, knowing whom, they declare, there is stoppage of birth."

If we can read these verses in Sanskrit, the vibrations of these tunes, by themselves, produce a calmness of mind, which, when taken to its logical conclusion, can bring about that stillness and tranquility, which centres one in the centre of one's heart, where the in-dwelling Supreme Reality is seen face to face, or is experienced.

The expounders of that Supreme Brahman proclaim Him to be eternal which means there is no birth and death for that Supreme Being. It remains forever and is all-pervading in the manifold world, and, in the hearts of all beings. And surrendering and settling oneself in that centre of consciousness, one attains perfect tranquility and freedom which is known as *nirvana*; it is known as *kaivalya*; it is known as *sahaja avastah*; it is known as that from which there is no return. It is this, which the Upanishads speak of; it is that perfect, unconditional, absolute freedom – *moksha,* which we all seek in understanding the Upanishads.

Aum shantih shantih shantihi!

Mundaka Upanishad

Some of the important teachings which have come to us from ancient times, were stated for the first time in the Mundaka Upanishad, over two thousand years ago. For instance, *satyameva jayate*: "Truth Alone Wins" – comes from the Mundaka Upanishad.

The other famous statement from the Mundaka Upanishad, which Swami Vivekananda was very fond of, is *naayam atmaa balaheenena labhya*: "This *atma* cannot be attained by the weak." There is a tendency among certain people to think that the Upanishads and Vedanta are only meant for people who have no other work to do, or, for those who cannot fight opposing forces and are weak-minded. In fact, they are meant for the strong as made clear by this statement.

The third important saying which most people do not even know comes from this ancient source, but often quote is, *andhenaiva niyamaana yatha andhaah,* which means, "the blind leading the blind." The Mundaka Upanishad discusses the state when a person, swollen with the pride of having read thousands of books, begins to lead people with just his bookish knowledge; that, the Upanishad says, is like "the blind leading the blind."

Mundaka also means "shaven-headed", so some people may misunderstand that this Upanishad is meant only for the *sanyasin* who has shaved his head. What it means is, to shave off ignorance and make the mind clear.

This Upanishad comes from the Atharva Veda. In fact, the lineage is mentioned: this Upanishad started from Atharvan, who is the son of Brahma. Let us now we take up the study of the Mundaka Upanishad.

There are people who think all this is meant for either *sanyasins* or people who have no interest in life and have retired to the forest: they are mistaken. The basic teaching of the Upanishads is how to find true happiness. Therefore, for those who feel that they have everything in life, and yet there is some vacuum somewhere and something is missing; for every such person, it would be very useful to start the study of the Upanishads. The reason why the Upanishads were not taught publicly, for a long time, was because many of the *rishis* felt that if they were to be improperly understood, they could create more problems than offer solutions. And perhaps there were also some who had vested interest in not letting everybody know what the Upanishads were all about.

In fact, when Buddha started preaching, some people felt uncomfortable because he was giving the essence of the Upanishads. When Adi Shankaracharya started teaching the Upanishads and opposing the Buddhists, those who were interested only in rituals and ceremonies, called him *prachchanna boudhika* or a "Buddhist in disguise" because they feared they would lose their hold.

The Upanishad is therefore a very profound teaching, to understand which, one has to give complete attention.

Part 1: SECTION 1

SHLOKA 1

Om brahmaa devaanaam prathamah sambabhoova
vishvasya kartaa bhuvanasya goptaa
sa brahmavidyaam sarvavidyaa pratishthaam
atharvaaya jyesthaputraaya praaha

The Mundaka Upanishad first gives a description of how the knowledge was passed down, where it started, the genesis of the Upanishad. It says:

Om brahmaa devaanaam prathamah sambabhoova vishwasya kartaa bhuvanasya goptaa – "First *Brahma* arose, the first among the Gods, the creator, the maker of the universe, the protector of the world."

sa brahmavidyaam sarvavidyaa pratishtaam – "Then he taught the knowledge of Brahman." What kind of knowledge? *sarvavidya pratishtaam* – "That which is the foundation of all knowledge." It is called the "foundation of all knowledge" because it is "that knowledge which, when known, nothing else remains to be known." It is the foundation of one's own true origin, of what one really is. *Atharvaaya jyestaputraaya praaha* – "To his eldest son, Atharvan, Brahma taught this knowledge."

SHLOKA 2

atharvane yaam pravadeta brahma atharvaa taam
purovaachaangire brahmavidyaam
sa bhaaradvaajaaya satyavaahaaya praaha
bhaaradvaajongirase paraavaraam

atharvane yaam pravadeta brahma atharvaa taam purovaachaangire brahmavidyaam – "That knowledge of Brahman, which Brahma taught to Atharvan; Atharvan, in the ancient times, taught to Angirasa." (A character is mentioned here named Angirasa) *sa bhaaradvaajaaya satyavaahaaya praaha bhaaradvaajongirase paraavaraam* – "Then he, Angirasa, taught it to Satyavaaha, who was the son of Bhaaradvaaja, and then the son of Bhaaradvaaja taught it to Angirasa." This is another Angirasa.

In the Vedas, there are different people at different times with the same name. "Vyasa" for instance means, "a compiler". So "Veda Vyasa" means "a compiler of Vedas". There could be many Vyasas – "compilers" – because in Sanskrit, every noun is formed from a verb. It is not a meaningless word. So Angirasa taught it to Satyavaaha. "Satyavaaha was the son of Bhaaradvaaja and he taught it to Angirasa again." What did he teach? *paraavaraam* – "He taught the *paraa aparaa*," which means he taught two kinds of knowledge – "the knowledge of the higher and of the lower."

SHLOKA 3

shaunako ha vai mahaashaalongirasam
vidhivad upasannah papraccha
kasmin nu bhagavo vijnaate sarvam
idam vijnaatam bhavati iti

Then, "Shaunaka, the great householder, approached Angirasa..." It is clear from this, that the Upanishad is not meant only for *sanyasins*; it was taught to "Shaunaka, the great householder".

Why "great householder" and not an ordinary one? If you read the ancient laws of how the householder should live, then you will understand the meaning of "great". For instance, one of the rules is when the food has been prepared, the householder is supposed to go out to the gate and loudly proclaim thrice, "Is anybody going hungry here?" If somebody answers, he has to be brought in and fed and the ideal householder should eat what is leftover. This is just an example. The householder happened to be the support of the entire system. Even the *sanyasin* had to be fed by the householder.

"Shaunaka, the great householder, duly approached Angirasa." "Duly" means, with all the respect that is necessary. He did not go to Angirasa and say, "Hey, teach me the knowledge of Brahman!" With great respect, with great understanding, Shaunaka approached Angirasa and asked him, *kasmin nu bhagavo vijnaate sarvam idam vijnaatam bhavati iti* – "Angirasa, I offer my *pranaam* to you. I bow down to you. Please tell me, what is that knowledge, venerable Sir. What is that which, when known, all this becomes known?"

This does not mean that the "knower of Brahman" will be an expert in engineering or mining or anything of that kind. The real interpretation of *sarvamidam vijnaatam bhavati iti* is, when That is known, the essence of oneself and the essence of the world is known and therefore, nothing else needs to be known.

It is not as if "everything" will be known when the knowledge of the Supreme Being is attained, but, one would have, by then, attained an excellent level of concentration which, when applied to any subject, makes it graspable and one can learn it faster than anybody else. But, the meaning here is not that when you know That, you know everything else!

SHLOKA 4

tasmai sa hovaacha- dve vidye veditavye iti ha sma yad
brahmavido vadanti paraa chaivaparaa cha

tasmai sa hovaacha – "He said to him…" *dve vidye veditavye iti ha sma yad brahmavido vadanti* – "Two kinds of knowledge are to be known, so say the knowers of Brahman."

What are the two kinds of knowledge? *paraa cha iva aparaa cha* – "The *paraa vidya* and the *aparaa vidya.* "The higher knowledge" and "the lower knowledge".

There is a very interesting list in the Mundaka Upanishad of what is *paraa vidya* or higher knowledge and what is *aparaa vidya* or lower knowledge. First, the *rishi* gives a list of what is part of the lower knowledge, *apaara vidya*:

SHLOKA 5

tatraaparaa rigvedo yajurvedah
saamavedotharavedah shikshaa
kalpo vyaakaranam niruktam chando jyotisham iti
atha paraa yayaa tad aksharam adhigamyate

This is the list of what is lower knowledge – "The *Rigveda, Yajurveda, Samaveda, Atharvaveda,* phonetics, ritual, grammar, etymology, metrics and astrology." *Jyotisha* need not necessarily mean astrology – it could also be astronomy. As a Vedanga, it is astronomy – knowledge of the heavens. All these are *aparaa vidya.*

Why does the *rishi* say, "All these are lower knowledge?" It is because he explains what the higher knowledge is, and compared to that higher knowledge, all this is lower knowledge. But that does not mean that one can ignore the study of the Upanishads just because they are *aparaa vidya*! *Aparaa vidya* is that which leads one to *paraa vidya.*

But while studying, one must remember that it is not just through reading and memorising all the Vedas, that one can know that Supreme Being. The Supreme Being can be known only through understanding and that is what the Upanishad teaches.

Therefore, all these are essential, but they are considered to be lower knowledge in comparison to the higher knowledge, which is the realisation of the Supreme Being.

In Bhaja Govindam, Shankaracharya said, "*nahi nahi rakshati dukrin karane*" – By going into the intricacies of grammar, one cannot see that Supreme Being. He went a step further and called everybody fools – *moodah matey*. This, the Upanishad has not done yet! It will come later in the Mundaka Upanishad.

Then, what is that higher knowledge? It is that by which the Undecaying, the Indestructible is apprehended: *atha paraa yayaa tad aksharam adhigamyate.*

The *rishis* said everything absolutely clearly. They were not fence-sitters. They declared everything in as clear terms as possible. Here, the *rishi* has described what is *aparaa vidya* and *paraa vidya*. After saying that the higher knowledge or *paraa vidya* is "That by which the Undecaying, the Indestructible is understood or apprehended" he then describes the so-called "qualities" of that Indestructible Supreme Being, Brahman, which has to be apprehended. And the description is:

SHLOKA 6

yat tad adreshyam agraahyam agotram avarnam
achakshuh shrotram tad apaani paadam
nityam vibhum sarvagatam susukshmam tad avyayam
yad bhootayonim paripashyanti dheeraah

This means, that the higher knowledge by which that Supreme Being is perceived and apprehended, is first described as *adreshyam,* that which cannot be seen: *adreshyam agraahyam agotram avarnam.*

It is *agraahyam* – "ungraspable". One may ask, "If It is ungraspable, then what is the use of studying the Upanishad?" What they mean by "ungraspable" is, that which cannot be grasped by the senses or by the ordinary, rational mind. It cannot be caught through reason, nor can It be grasped by the senses. If It could be grasped by reasoning, then the most intelligent person would also be "the knower of Brahman" which is not the case generally! In these matters, we are talking of a different dimension altogether and sometimes, two and two can become five!

It is *agotram,* which means, it does not have a particular caste. We can also say "no origin". That means, "That which does not belong to one particular family or lineage."

It is *avarnam,* which means "It is without colour."

It is *achakshuh shrotram* – "It is without sight or hearing. It does not have eyes or ears like ours."

It is apaani paadam – "without hands or feet."

It is "eternal", *nityam,* because It is "That which remains always when everything else disappears." Therefore, one of the most important features of that Supreme Being is that It is *nitya* – "That which remains forever, permanent"; as opposed to the impermanence of the things that we see around us.

Then, "*vibhum sarvagatam susukshmam tad avyayam yad bhootayonim paripashyanti dheeraah*" – "It is Eternal, All-pervading, Omnipresent, exceedingly Subtle (*susukshman*)". "Subtler than the subtlest" is one of the descriptions given in the Upanishad – "That which is so subtle that It cannot be grasped even by the mind." The Kenopanishad says, "*yen manasa na manute yen ahur mano matam*" – "That which even the mind cannot grasp, but because of which the mind exists."

"*Bhootayonim paripashyanti dheeraah*" – "That, the wise perceive as the Source of all beings." "Wise" meaning "Those who have understood That Supreme Being as the Source of everything in this universe." All this comes from That Supreme Being. "*Bhootayonim*" – "Source of all the *bhoota* (elements)."

The world, or the universe, and how it came about are mentioned in the next *shloka.* It says:

SHLOKA 7

yathornanaabhih srijate grihnate cha
yathaa prithivyaam oshadhayas sambhavanti
yathaa sataha purushaat keshalomaani
tathaaksharaat sambhavateeha vishvam

The Upanishad gives the example of a spider, which takes out some material from itself when it builds its web, and then draws it back again. So, "Just as the spider sends forth its cobweb and draws it back; just as herbs grow on this earth..." – The herbs grow naturally; nobody does anything to them – "...just as hair grows on the head and body of a living person, in the same way, from the Imperishable arises this entire universe, naturally."

SHLOKA 8

tapasaa cheeyate brahma tatonnam abhijaayate
annaat praano manah satyam lokaah karmasu cha amritam

Brahman, the Supreme Being expands, grows. In fact, the root of the word, Brahman, is *brih,* "to expand". "That Supreme Being Brahman expands." How does He expand? By *tapasya,* "contemplation". Therefore, it implies that any kind of expansion, any kind of growth, any kind of moving into higher things, can also be attained through *tapasya*. In the Upanishad, it is described in different ways and one of the descriptions of *tapasya* is "sacrifice", which means the capacity to go into hardship and do penance to achieve your aim.

Even the expansion of the universe comes through the *tapasya* or penance or austerities of the Supreme Being. "From that *tapasya* of the Supreme Being, first comes nourishment" – *annam* here means "nourishment". It does not mean just the food that we eat; it means nourishment. "And from there, comes the mind; then come the five elements", which are mentioned as the *pancha bhoota.* And then, from the five elements come, "the combination of the five elements, which makes the world, and once the world is created, comes the different rituals that we perform and from there, the resulting immortality." "Ritual" also means "the practice of living" which itself is a ritual.

SHLOKA 9

yah sarvajnah sarvavid yasya jnaanamayam tapah
tasmaad etad brahma naama roopam annam cha jaayate

A particular kind of *tapasya* is described. "He is All-knowing", who has understood that Supreme, "who is the Brahman", that Supreme Reality, who is not only All-knowing but also *sarvavid* (All-wise);whose austerity or *tapasya* consists of knowledge; *jnaanamayam tapah;* for whom *tapasya* is knowledge itself, or, "the understanding of knowledge is his *tapasya.* From that Brahman, from that Supreme Being is born this Brahma."

This means that from that unconditioned Supreme Being is born this conditioned being called Brahma, who is the creator, who is also mentioned as *hiranyagarbha.*

"*Naamaroopam annam cha jaayate*" – "And from that is also born name, shape and form and their nourishment."

To put it in a nutshell, from that undifferentiated Supreme Reality come all these different forms with their names and shapes, and also the nourishment that they need. From that undifferentiated Supreme Reality come the differentiated names, the diversity that we see, which have various names and forms, and are nourished by what they need.

Now, to look at it in the opposite way: Each thing that we see here in this world, which is nourished, is with *naama-rupa* and ultimately, when it is free of the difference of name and form, it goes back to the Source, or the undifferentiated Supreme Being. And that is the journey – from diversity to Unity. This is the Upanishadic teaching: to go back from the differences to the Single, to go back from diversity to Unity, to trace back one's Source and come to understand that one is a "spark" of that Supreme Reality, which the Upanishads call Brahman.

This is section I of the Mundaka Upanishad.

In the next section of the Mundaka, there is a description of what is known as "ceremonial religion", which means "rituals".

Some people who say, "Since we are studying the Upanishads, we do not need to go into all this", take the Upanishad's antipathy to rituals to an extreme. This is a totally wrong interpretation of these matters because "ritual" does not mean merely a ceremony. The word "ritual" means "any activity which is repeated regularly."

What the Upanishad is against is that one must not just stick to the skeleton, the shell of the ritual; one must find out what the deep meaning of it is and go into it. Before one touches that meaning, before one becomes free, before one has attained a stage of maturity to understand the Truth, it is sometimes very essential to follow certain rituals, to follow a certain path, because each individual is made differently.

One individual in a million may be able to go directly to the Truth, but we cannot imitate. Each person has his or her own pace. In many cases, it is necessary to follow a certain path, certain rituals. If before starting, one says, "Truth is a pathless land", one will end up pathless!

Certain rituals, certain direction, certain attention, a certain path are necessary, before you arrive at that stage of maturity; that will now be discussed in the Mundaka.

Part 1: SECTION 2

In Part I Section II, the *rishi* describes what is known as "ceremonial religion". As one proceeds or starts from a point, that aspect of religion called rituals are to be followed by most, so that the attention is fixed on the path.

SHLOKA 1

Tad etat satyam mantreshu karmani kavayo
yaany apashyams taani tretaayaam bahudhaa santataani
taanya acharatha niyatam satyakaamaa
esha vah panthaah sukritasya loke

tad etat satyam – "That is the Truth." This is meant for those who are "lovers of Truth", whose main desire is for the Truth, whose only priority is to find the Truth – the "Satyakaama". Normally, our priorities are all mixed up. We get time for everything, but for meditation we do not get time as we do not give it priority.

The *rishi* says, "This is the Truth. The activities, the works that the sages have mentioned in the different hymns of the Vedas – perform them constantly, if you are "lovers of Truth". You lovers of Truth, perform the actions prescribed by the sages who have understood the Vedas. Continue to perform them until you have found the Truth. This is your path to the world of good deeds. Perform them, and you will reach the path of the Supreme Truth."

The word "ritual" here describes any activity, which is done by one externally, in the external world, and that which is done internally by the one who moves towards the Truth.

SHLOKA 2

yathaa lelaayate hy archih
samiddhe havyavaahane
tad aajyabhaagaavantarenaahutih
pratipaadayet shraddhayaahutam

Now, the *rishi* describes the fire-sacrifice, the *homa,* in which the fire burns. He says, "When the flame moves, after the fire has been kindled, then one should pour, with faith, his oblations of melted butter, between the two portions of the fire." How does one pour it? Not as a mere ritual but "with faith" saying, "Here, I offer myself into the fire. Here, I sacrifice my all into the fire."

To ask an ordinary person to sacrifice everything to find the Truth is a tall order. He begins, first, by offering oblations into the fire. A person, who is not interested, would rather eat the oblations than offer them!

One has to make a start and proceed slowly. One cannot take giant leaps in this field.

SHLOKA 3

yasyaagnihotram adarsham apaurnamaasam
achaaturmaasyam anaagrayanam atithivarjitam cha
ahutam avaishvadevam avidhinaa hutam
aasaptamaams tasya lokaan hinasti

"If a person's fire-sacrifice or *agnihotra* is not followed by the other rules which are to be followed, like the sacrifice of the new moon, the full moon, *chaaturmaasya*" – which means the "sacrifice of the four months" and other prescribed rituals – "he will be without guests, without oblations, without the ceremony, to all Gods, or gives offerings contrary to rule; and destroys his worlds till the seventh."

One need not worry about the number "seven" – it means, if one does not follow the rules of practice, laid down by the *rishis,* to find the Truth, then one "destroys all the seven worlds that are to follow", which means, one suffers in all the stages of progress towards the Supreme Being.

Listen carefully, understand, try to follow what has been prescribed by the *rishis.* Do not throw everything overboard because you have read the Upanishads! Certain regulations and rules have to be followed to progress. We know what happens when we say, "All this is nonsense"! There is chaos.

So, provided you are a "lover of Truth", follow whatever practices have been prescribed by the teacher depending on what is suitable to you. This can be found only by consulting a person who knows about it. If a great teacher with whom you have contact and dialogue, says, "All this is not necessary for you – this and this is enough", then, you can follow that. But do not make your own decisions regarding the matter because some rituals may be very useful to you in your progress, on your path. Of course, when you have reached the end of it, you can drop everything.

That is what the *sanyasin* does, when he does the *viraja homa* and takes *sanyasa*: he cuts his sacred thread and puts it into the fire. He has no caste after that; he cuts off his tuft to indicate that he has no family. For such a person, there is no need of any ritual. But we are not so: we think we are free, but, we are free of one set of rituals and caught in another. Rules and regulations are made so that we are caught in something that is useful and will take us further on our path.

Then, there is a description of "the seven moving flames of fire". The *rishi,* the person who performs the sacrifice, watches the fire and sees different kinds of flames in the *homa kunda.*

The different kinds of flames in the fire-ritual, *agnihotra,* are described thus:

SHLOKA 4

kaalii karalii cha manojavaa cha
sulohitaa yaa cha sudhoomravarnaa
sphulinginii vishvaroopii cha devii
lelaayamaanaa iti sapta jihvaah

"There are the seven tongues of fire. The black, the terrific, the swift as mind, the very red, the very smoky-coloured, the spark of the fire, the all-shaped goddess."

Now all of a sudden, after talking about abstractions, we have come to the "all-shaped goddess"; to the "spark of the fire"; to the different forms of the flames: "the black", "the terrific", "the swift as mind", "the red", and the "the smoky-coloured". This could be the description of the different kinds of flames in the fire-sacrifice.

But, if you go to a teacher who is personally into the practice of a certain *marga,* he/she will help you to identify all these colours and fires with the different centres of consciousness – the *chakras* – which also happen to be seven. Such a teacher will tell you how the consciousness or the Energy is worshipped as a goddess – the "all-shaped goddess" – but, we will not go into it now.

We will consider this, at the moment, as a description of the "fire of *agnihotra*" and "the seven kinds of flames".

SHLOKA 5

eteshu yashcharate bhraajamaaneshu
yathaakaalam chaahutay hy aadadaayan
tam nayanty etas sooryasya rashmayo
yatra devaanaam patir ekodhivaasah

"If you perform the works which have been prescribed by the *rishis,* and, according to their instructions, make offerings at the proper time when these tongues are shining, then these offerings, in the form of the rays of the sun, lead you to the world where that Supreme Being resides."

SHLOKA 6

ehy eheeti tam aahutayas suvarchasah
sooryasya rashmibhir yajamaanam vahanti
priyaam vaacham abhivadantyorchayantya
esha vah punyas sukrito brahmalokah

The offerings which you have made, the sacrifices which you have done to attain that abode of the Supreme Being, all that you have given – "Those offerings will come in the form of hosts, and they will receive you, saying, 'Come, come!' They will carry the sacrificer by the rays of the sun, honoring him and saluting him with pleasing words, saying, 'This is the holy World of Brahma, won through good deeds!'"

After describing the sacrifices, the *agnihotra* and so on, the Upanishad makes a subtle shift in the seventh *shloka*. It says:

SHLOKA 7

plavaa hy ete adridhaa yajnaroopaa
ashtaadashoktam avaram yeshu karmaa
etacchreyo yebhinandanti moodhaah
jaraamrityum te punar evaapiyanti

plavaa hy ete adridhaa yajnaroopaa ashtaadashoktama varam yeshu karma – "Unsteady are these boats of the eighteen sacrificial forms, which are said to be inferior *karma.*" This means that while it is necessary for you to follow a path and do certain rituals which have been prescribed, it could be that what you are performing is "the inferior path", the lower knowledge.

They are called the "eighteen sacrificial forms" because, for the *agnihotra,* there are sixteen *ritviks* who sit down for the sacrifice along with the *yajamana,* the sacrificer, and his wife. For every sacrifice, the wife is necessary to perform, what is known as *ashtadashoktam,* the "eighteen-fold sacrifice".

But, even that could be "the inferior *karma*", because, *etacchreyo yehbhinandanti moodhaah jaraamrityum te punar evaapi yanti* – "the deluded" – those who are caught in the illusion – "delight in this, which they have done, as leading to good; but fall again into old age and death."

SHLOKA 8

avidyaayaam antare vartamaanaah svayam
dheeraah panditam manyamaanaah
janghanyamaanaah pariyanti moodaah
andhenaiva neeyamaanaa yatha andhaah

The Upanishad says about such people, "They abide in the midst of ignorance, wise in their own esteem, thinking themselves to be learned, but they are fools, afflicted with troubles", because they think that the be-all and end-all of happiness is this world and all that is done is for goodness in *this* world, for happiness in *this* world. They do not think of the other.

"Such people, abiding in the midst of ignorance, wise in their own esteem" – nobody calls them wise but they think that they are wise – "thinking themselves to be learned" – *svayam dheeraah panditam manyamaanaa* – "but, they are fools afflicted with troubles, who are not only under illusion themselves, but they also lead others into illusion."

So how do they go about doing that? *andhenaiva neeyamaanaa yatha andhaah* – "Like the blind leading the blind." So this expression, "blind leading the blind", is, at least, by a conservative estimate, two thousand years old; it is not new! It was not invented by the English dictionary!

SHLOKA 9

avidyaayaam bahudhaa vartamaanaa
vayam kritaartha ity abhimanyanti baalaah
yat karmino na pravedayanti raagaat
tenaaturaah ksheenalokaaschyavante

These deluded men are called "the immature". They have not come to the full evolution of their consciousness or their intelligence. "The immature, living in ignorance, think that by performing the rituals, 'We have achieved our aim; we have accomplished our aim'. They do not understand the Truth because of *raaga* (attachments). Therefore, they sink down, wretched, when their merits are exhausted."

We need not even think of other worlds; we can see what happens in this world. We are attached to so many things in life. We think we have achieved our happiness by acquiring that which we are attached to. Then what happens after a while? We grow old and we cannot enjoy it anymore, or, just as we are about to enjoy, we may drop dead or that which we are attached to, is taken away from us. So where is the happiness? What happens then? We sink down, feel wretched.

This also applies, if you believe in future births, to other worlds, because here, the implication is also that those who perform sacrifices, who think auspiciously, who do good deeds, who help others and so on go to higher worlds. But when the merit is exhausted, they come back again to this world and lead a miserable existence.

SHLOKA 10

ishtaapoortam manyamaanaa varishtam
naanyacchreyo vedayante pramoodhaah
naakasya prishthe te sukritenubhootvemam
lokam heenataram vaa vishanti

"These deluded men, regarding sacrifices and works of merit as most important, do not know any other good." They think that sacrifices and good works are the most important thing – they do not know anything beyond that. "Having enjoyed in heaven, the high place won by good deeds, they enter this world again or may be a still lower one."

It is obvious that the Upanishad and the ancient Vedic philosophy believe in birth after birth, or the transmigration of the soul. Therefore, it says, even if you enjoy the effect of your good deeds in heaven or in some other higher plane, you come back again into this world or perhaps into a still lower world, because you are caught, attached and drawn towards it.

Sometimes people ask, "Can human beings be born as animals?" We really cannot tell you clearly whether it is possible or not. But, I can tell you one thing: there are many who are born as human beings but are with animal characteristics.

There is a story of the great Saint Nizamudin, who lived in Delhi. He used to go for the Friday prayers with a blind-fold over his eyes. He was once asked, "Why do you wear a blind-fold?" He said, "Does anybody want to try it?" The story says that someone volunteered and tried the blind-fold, looked around and saw that most of the people, who had gathered for worship in the mosque, had animal faces! Some looked like pigs, some like dogs and some like other animals. He said, "What is happening? They are on the outside like humans but inside they are not!" So, "lower birth" and "animal birth" could also mean "animal instincts" and "animal life". Sometimes you find animals that are as good as humans or even better!

The deluded men who regard sacrifice and works of merit as the most important, enjoy for a while and then get back into the same world or perhaps into a lower world – that is about the ordinary sacrificers whose only interest is happiness in this world.

If you need happiness in this world, you still need to sacrifice, you have to work hard. If you do not work hard for the exams, you are not going to get good marks. Or, if you want to make money, you have to sacrifice something. Thus, sacrifice is essential.

Till now, the condition of those who sacrifice for material pleasures and happiness was mentioned. The Upanishad never says "Do not do that!" *dharma artha kaama* and *moksha* are all legitimate.

In the next *shloka,* the *rishi* talks about those who perform another kind of sacrifice, who go steadily on to the understanding of the Supreme Truth and eternal happiness.

SHLOKA 11

Tapah shraddhe ye hy upavasanty aranye
shantaa vidvaamso bhaiksh acharyaam charantah
sooryadvaarena te virajaah prayaanti
yatraamritah sa purusho hy avyayaatmaa

"Those who practice austerity and faith in forests, those tranquil knowers, who live the life of mendicants in forests, depart, free from sin, through the orb of the sun, to where the Immortal, Imperishable Person dwells."

Those who have sacrificed everything else for the understanding of the Supreme Truth, therefore, practice austerity or *tapas;* they also have *shraddha* (faith) and they live in forests or in quiet places. They want to find out what the Truth is. Such persons, instead of enjoying for a while the results of their good deeds and then coming back again to a miserable existence, go higher and higher into happiness, until they reach the abode of that Supreme Being, who, by His very essence, is Bliss. There is no more of this "coming and going". It stops, because their sacrifice is one of austerity and faith.

After having said that, the Upanishad describes the Truth, that Supreme Being, who is absolute Bliss, who is free. When That is attained, one is free of all misery and when That is known, "nothing more remains to be known".

How is that Supreme Being to be attained? How does one approach that Supreme Being? It cannot be found out by reading; but as the *rishi* has said, "through *tapasya* and through *shraddha*". Apart from that, there are other ways to find out, for which you need a guide. In fact, even to practice ordinary things like *yogasanas,* it is better to take guidance from a teacher because you may tie yourself in a knot from which you cannot come out!

So, a guide is essential. And to approach the Supreme Being is no ordinary thing. It is very subtle. It is the absolute essence of happiness, the essence of life, the true meaning of life, and for attaining That, you need instructions, you need guidance.

The next *shloka* describes how to find the Supreme Being, whom to approach and what to do.

SHLOKA 12

pareekshya lokaan karmachitaan braahmano
nirvedam aayaan nasty akritah kritena
tad vijnaanaartham sa gurum evaabhigacchet
samitpaanih shrotriyam brahmanishtam

There are some qualifications of an aspirant that are first described; only such an aspirant will start looking for the Truth and for the instructions to find It. The *rishi* gives the qualifications of an aspirant – the seeker of the Truth – and then, the qualifications of a teacher who is qualified to guide.

"The seeker is one who has seen the worlds won by good deeds and also the utter futility and emptiness of the achievements of this world." He has seen how happiness is such a short-lived experience. How nobody is completely happy, how, in any happiness, there is always some unhappiness hidden, which, at any moment, can show up.

Having seen this uncertainty and the futility of finding happiness in the worlds won by *karma*, by works in this world, the Upanishad says, "Let a *brahmana* arrive at non-attachment." A *brahmana* here means "one who is intent upon knowing the Brahman" – *brahma vit brahma aiva bhavati.*

Seeing the futility of attachment in this world, and understanding that non-attachment is "not being caught by this world", this state has to awaken in the mind of a seeker, at least, to some extent, if he is going to seriously enquire into the knowledge of Brahman. The Upanishad will not penetrate, however much we talk, unless and until one understands the impermanence of this world,

Somewhere along the line, when man, by his experience, realises the futility of this whole circus that is going on, and sees how people respect you when you are rich and kick you when you are poor; how there is no true love or affection between people and that it is only a question of exploiting each other; seeing all this – the sufferings of this world with just snatches of joy – he arrives at non-attachment.

And having understood the impermanence of the world and getting the notion, in the back of his mind, that "there must be some way out of this mess" he or she should approach a teacher as *samitpaani* or one with the "sacrificial-fuel" in hand. "For the sake of understanding the true knowledge, which leads one to eternal happiness, the student should approach a *guru,* who should be a *shrotriya,* or "learned in the scriptures" and a *brahmanishta,* (established in the Brahman), bringing *samit* in hand."

Bringing this *samit* (sacrificial fuel) in hand to the teacher has many meanings: One is that it is a symbol to demonstrate that the student is ready to sacrifice everything for understanding that Truth. If such a student approaches a teacher who is qualified, then the deed is done. If it is a half-hearted attempt, then naturally, it will take time. The other meaning is that by taking the "sacrificial-fuel" to the teacher, the student shows that he is ready to sacrifice even the "sacrificial-fuel" that was given to him when he got married. He is sacrificing everything to the *guru.*

But what kind of *guru* should he go to? The Upanishad says that the *guru* must have two qualifications: one is that he is "established in Brahman" or is a *brahmanishta,* and the other is that he is "learned in the scriptures" or *shrotriya.* This combination is hard to get. Some people are *shrotriya* but not *brahmanishta.* If there is a combination of both in a person, then he is an ideal teacher.

The Upanishads and the Vedas are *shruti* – they are the experiences and the revelations that have come to people who have gone into the Truth. So if one is a *shrotriya,* and if he has a spiritual experience, he knows where he stands because it has all been done before, it is nothing new. So, when he reaches a certain stage of spiritual illumination, he knows the points of reference. He knows where he stands.

He does not think, "I have attained everything and therefore, throw all the books into the river!" We hear that very often! He knows where he has reached, because, in this particular journey, there are many "stations" – the *sufis* call them, *mukhaam*. And each station is blissful and feels wonderful; and, compared to the stage from which you have come, it appears that you have attained everything!

But if you are a *shrotriya,* if you have read the *shruti,* you will see that these are all different stages to the Highest. So it is a point of reference. Therefore, as Swami Vivekananda used to say that if a person says he has realised the Absolute Truth and at the same time says, "All the scriptures are nonsense" be careful! Take it with a pinch of salt.

So go to a teacher who is both a *shrotriya* and a *brahmanishta.* But, what is the condition to go to the teacher? That you should be a *satya-kaama* – your desire, your priority is to know the Truth. You are ready to sacrifice everything to understand the Truth and with that intention and one-pointedness, you must approach a *guru* who is a *bhramanishta* himself, who has knowledge of Brahman, who has realised Brahman, who is also a *shrotriya* himself.

SHLOKA 13

tasmai sa vidvaan upasannaaya samyak
prashaanta chittaaya samaanvitaaya
yenaaksharam purusham veda satyam
provaacha taam tattvato brahmavidyaam

"Unto him who has thus approached, in due form, in the right manner possible, whose mind is tranquil, who has attained peace, let the knowing teacher teach *Brahma vidya.*"

Do not go to such a teacher and say, "Hey you! Can you teach me the Truth?" Approach him in due form and with great respect. When the qualified student, whose mind is tranquil and has attained peace, approaches the "knowing" teacher – not *andhaah,* "the blind leader" – but the teacher who really knows; let such a teacher teach the very truth about *Brahman* by which one comes to know the Imperishable Person, who is the Truth. That is *Brahma vidya.*

Part 2: SECTION 1

SHLOKA 1

tad etat satyam yathaa sudeeptaat paavakaad
visphulingaah sahasrashah prabhavante saroopaah
tatha aksharaad vividhaah saumya bhaavaah
prajaayante tatra chaivaapi yanti

What does the teacher say? "This is the Truth: just as sparks come out of the blazing fire by the thousands, even so, many kinds of beings come forth from the Immutable Supreme and then they return to It."

The "sparks" that come out of the "blazing fire" are also only fire – they are part of the fire and cannot be distinguished, as they are the same. Here, "the blazing fire" is equated with the Supreme Being, *Brahman,* and "the sparks" are equated with the *atman,* the individual beings, who are in this world. Before the "sparks" return to the "blazing fire", the interim stage is what we are in now – the return has to take place at some time. But the *rishi* says, "If you know that one has to ultimately return, why wait? Go back immediately to 'the blazing fire'! Why do you want to be a mere 'spark'?"

What I want to point out, especially, is the way in which the seeker is addressed by the teacher as *saumya,* or "beloved one". The teacher does not say, "You idiot, listen to me!" He says, "O beloved one", which shows that the connection between the teacher and the student is one of great love and affection. That love and affection comes only through proper understanding. Such a great, spiritual teacher, who is a *brahmanishta,* is full of compassion in his heart.

That is why, if I am practising what is known as *sadhana,* which is supposed to take me closer and closer to the Supreme Being, and if, after twenty years of such *sadhana,* I have various visions but my heart does not melt if I hear someone crying at my door, then there is something totally wrong with my *sadhana.* I have to go within and try to workout, "What is wrong with me? Where have I gone wrong?"

The closer one moves to the Supreme Being the softer the heart becomes, because you are also part of that Supreme Being and you realise that others are also "sparks" of that Supreme Being. So, when someone is hurt, you are hurt. If it does not happen, then there is something terribly wrong.

Since great spiritual teachers have deep affection, the student here is called, "O beloved one", *saumya.*

Then the *rishi* describes the Supreme Being again in different words. They are only different ways of trying to describe the Indescribable "blazing fire" or the Supreme Being.

SHLOKA 2

divyo hy amoortah purushah
sa baahyaabhyantaro hy ajah
apraano hy amanaah shubhro
aksharaat paratah parah

"Divine and formless is that Person, that Supreme Being. He is without and within, unborn, without breath, without mind, pure, higher than the highest, and immutable."

If you think of something as the highest, then He is higher than that, which means, the more the individual "spark" of that "blazing fire" begins to reflect on these characteristics of the Supreme Being, slowly and slowly, he moves closer to that Supreme Being.

And that Supreme Being is divine. He is within and without. He is "unborn" and "without breath". The Isha Vasya Upanishad also says the same thing in different words: *Isha vaasyam idam sarvam yat kim cha jagatyaam jagat* – "That Supreme *Isha* pervades everything here: that which moves and that which does not move." That is also the teaching given here.

SHLOKA 3

etasmajjaayate praano
manah sarvendriyaani cha
kham vaayur jyotir aapah
prithivee vishvasya dhaarinee

"From Him are born life, mind, all sense organs, *akasha*, air, light, water and earth, for He is the supporter of all." Or, it could also be translated as "earth, which is the supporter of all."

Then again, a graphic description is given, of the "Indescribable".

SHLOKA 4

agnir moordhaa chakshushee chandrasooryau
dishah shrotre vaag vivritaascha vedaah
vaayuh praano hridayam vishvam asya
padbhyaam prithivi hy esha sarva bhootaantaraatma

"Fire is His head; His eyes are the sun and the moon" – this is a figurative description. Do not think that the *rishis* were childish enough to think that the Supreme Being had the sun and the moon in the eyes! In fact, the *rishis* were very scientific because *jyotisha* is one of the *angaas* of the Vedas and astronomy was well developed.

In the olden days, people thought that art had to imitate nature. So they used to paint beautiful flowers. And the beauty was judged by saying, "Oh, how much like a real flower it looks!" Then came photography and no artist could do as perfect a duplication of nature as photography. Then it occurred to the artists that art should be more an expression of what our reaction to it is, rather than a duplication and imitation of nature.

Then modern art developed, as a movement, starting with Picasso. If you go to Puri, you will see Lord Jagannath, in the temple. There is nothing there except two stumps and round eyes to represent the Lord of the universe, Jagannath. It is one of the earliest abstract representations of "the all-seeing eyes". It is not childish art but a deliberate attempt.

In the same way, the artist's expression of exaggerated beauty is seen in ancient art – Chola art or Khajuraho and so on – in which all the parts of the human body that are normally associated with *rasa,* are exaggerated deliberately. It is not as if they did not know how to make the correct figure.

It is only through such expression that one can try to grasp what cannot be grasped.

Therefore, in the *shloka* the Supreme Being is symbolically described: "The fire is His head; His eyes are the sun and moon; the regions of space are His ears; His speech are the revealed Vedas; air is His life and His heart and the world. Out of His feet, the earth is born. Indeed, He is the Self of all beings" (*sarva bhootaantaraatma*).

SHLOKA 5

tasmaad agnir samidho yasya sooryah
somaat parjanya oshadhayah prithivyaam
pumaan retas sinchati yoshitaayaam
bahveeh prajaah purushaat samprasootaah

"From Him proceeds fire; from Him proceeds the sun, the moon, the rain, and the herbs on the earth; and, nourished by all this, the male-fire pours the seed in the female. Thus all creatures are produced from the Person."

SHLOKA 6

tasmaad richah saama yajoomshi deekshaa
yajnaas cha sarve kratavo dakshinaas cha
samvatsaras cha yajamaanas cha lokaah
somo yatra pavate yatra sooryah

"From Him are born the Rig Veda, the Sama, the Yajus, which means the formulae of sacrifice, the rites of initiation, all the sacrifices, ceremonies and the sacrificial gifts; the year, the sacrificer, the world where the moon purifies, where the sun shines."

This means, there is nothing here in this cosmos, which is not pervaded by that Supreme Being. From the Supreme Being proceeds everything. Therefore, our journey is to trace our Source and go back to that Supreme Being. This is the message.

SHLOKA 7

sapta praanaah prabhavanti tasmaat
saptaarchishah samidhas sapta homaah
sapta ime lokaa yeshu charanti praanaa
guhaashayaa nihitaas sapta sapta

"From Him comes forth the seven life-breaths, the seven flames, their fuel, the seven oblations, these seven worlds in which move the life-breaths and the seven which dwell in the secret place of the heart."

It says, in the end, *sapta ime lokaa yeshu charanti praanaa guhaa-shayaa nihitaah sapta sapta* – "These life-breaths that move in the seven places in the body and the seven worlds dwell in the secret place of the heart." "Heart" is not yet mentioned but it will be later on.

SHLOKA 8

atas samudraa girayas cha sarve asmaat
syandante sindhavas sarva roopaah
atas cha sarvaa oshadhayo rasas cha
yenaisha bhootais tishthate hy antaraatma

"From Him come all the seas and the mountains; from Him flow the rivers of every kind; from Him are all the herbs and their juices, by which, together with the elements, the inner Soul is held."

SHLOKA 9

purusha evedam vishvam
karma tapo brahma paraamritam
etad yo veda nihitam guhaayaam
sovidyaagranthim vikirateeha saumya

Again, the teacher calls the seeker, "O beloved one." "That Supreme Person is all this that we have described – austerity is He and that Brahman beyond death, is also Him. He who knows That, which is seated in the secret place, O beloved one, cuts off 'the knot of ignorance' here, on this earth."

That means, if you could only know, if you could only realise that the "spark" in you is really a part of that "blazing fire" from which everything proceeds, which is Absolute and Supreme, then "the knot of ignorance" is cut. No more will you think that you are identified with this little ego and fall repeatedly in this circuit of birth, death and suffering.

Part 2: SECTION 2

SHLOKA 1

aavih sannihitam guhaacharam naama
mahat padam atraitat samarpitam
ejat praanan nimishaccha yad etajjaanatha sad asad varenyam
param vijnaanaad yad varishhtam prajaanaam

"Manifest, well-fixed, moving, dwelling in the secret place of the heart – such is the great support." "Support" here means the Supreme Being, Brahman.

"In It, is centred all that moves, breathes and winks. Know that as Being, as well as non-being". It is also "non-being" as It cannot be identified with the limited being.

"Know that to be the Supreme Object to be desired. It is the highest, beyond the reach of man's understanding." No amount of intellectual arguments, no amount of cerebration can lead one to that Supreme Being. It is beyond the scope of man's understanding.

If It is beyond the scope of man's understanding, how does one understand It? It will be described later. But let us mention it a little earlier that when the intellect, meaning the mind and the brain, has through constant reasoning and reading of the scriptures, understood that by no amount of grasping and by no amount of effort is it possible for it to attain that dimension of the Supreme Being, then, it gives up and settles down. No more does it move from this direction to that direction or from that direction to this.

In that state of absolute stillness, which the *bhakta* calls "surrender", "something" takes place. What happens is that when complete stillness is in the mind, the individual ego has also subsided. "Fancy no more unfurls her wings." There is absolute stillness and in that, is the possibility of the understanding of the Supreme Being – neither through the senses can It be grasped, nor through the mind, which is very limited.

And therefore, *sadhana* is the way by which the instruments of perception, other than those of the senses and the mind, are opened up so that one goes closer to that Supreme Being. You need a microscope to look at even ordinary things like microbes. So too, we need other instruments of perception, faculties – other than the reasoning and the senses – to find that Supreme Being. Therefore, He is mentioned as "ungraspable". But if It can never be grasped, then there would be no point in our reading or understanding anything. But *sadhana* is the way by which other instruments of perception are opened.

SHLOKA 2

yad archimad yad anubhyonu cha
yasmin lokaa nihitaa lokinas cha
tad etad aksharam brahma sa praanas tad vaangmanah
tad etat satyam tad amritam tad veddhavyam saumya viddhi

"Understand, O beloved disciple, what is luminous, what is subtler than the subtlest, in which are centred all the worlds and those that dwell in them; That is the imperishable Supreme Brahman, That is life, That is speech and That is the mind, That is Truth, That is immortal and That is to be known – nothing else is to be known except That."

SHLOKA 3

dhanur grihitva auapanishadam mahaastram
sharam hy upaasaanishitam sandadheeta
aayamya tad bhaavagatena chetasaa
lakshyam tad evaaksharam saumya viddhi

"O beloved disciple, know that That 'imperishable' Supreme Being is the target. Use the great weapon, the Upanishads, as the bow and place in it the arrow which is sharpened by meditation, and draw it with the mind that is engaged in the contemplation of that Brahman."

"Take as the bow, the great weapon of the Upanishads, place in it the arrow sharpened by meditation" – not an ordinary arrow but that which is sharpened by *upasana,* by meditation – "draw it with a mind engaged in contemplation of that Brahman, O beloved one, and know that That 'imperishable' Brahman is your target."

SHLOKA 4

pranavo dhanuh sharo hy aatmaa
brahma tal lakshyam uchyate
apramattena veddhavyam
sharavat tanmayo bhavet

The syllable *aum* is the bow – "Use *aum* as the bow, one's inner Self as the arrow and Brahman is the target. It is to be hit without making a mistake. Thus one becomes united with It, as the arrow becomes one with the target."

This is the advice given of how to hit the target of Brahman. *Aum* is to be used as the bow. Further instruction in this matter, I think, should be taken from a teacher who is a *brahmanishta* and a *shrotriya*.

SHLOKA 5

yasmin dyauh prithivee cha antariksham otam
manah saha praanaischa sarvaih
tam evaikam jaanatha atmaanam anyaa
vaacho vimunchatha amritasyaisha setuh

dyauh is "sky"; *prithivee* is "earth", *antariksham* is "the space between". "He, in whom the sky, the earth and the inter-space are woven together..." "...and also the mind and all the vital breaths..." The *praana* is divided into *apaana, udaana, samaana, vyaana*; different kinds of life-energies that have been graded.

tamevaikam jaanatha aatmaanam – "That alone is the *atman*, understand."

anya vaacho vimunchathaa – "Dismiss other utterances." Forget about other things. Whatever other things I have said, neglect it. Just remember that the sky, the earth and that which is in between, the mind, the *prana;* they all come from that one Supreme Being. Remember only that. "Dismiss other utterances" for *amritasyaisha setuh* – "This is the bridge to immortality."

"Remember that and forget about other things." That means slowly begin to dissociate from your mind the idea that you are the body – "I am this", "I am that", "This is my body". Slowly, as one begins to dissociate oneself from this and dismisses it as utter nonsense, then "the bridge to immortality" is created and one marches on to that Supreme Being from which the whole circus has begun. Do not ask me why it has begun – I have no idea!

SHLOKA 6

araa iva rathanaabhau samhataa yatra naadyah
sa eshontas charate bahudhaa jaayamaanah

aum ity evam dhyaayatha aatmaanam
svasti vah paaraaya tamasah parastaat

"Where the arteries of the body are brought together like the spokes in the centre of a wheel…" "Arteries" need not necessarily mean the physical arteries – it could also mean all the pathways through which energy travels. Just as in the wheel, the center is the point where all the spokes are brought together, so too, in the body, the arteries are brought together in the centre, and "… within that Centre is the Self. Meditate on that *aum* as Self."

Then the prayer is, "May you be successful in crossing over to the further shore beyond darkness." That means, In the *hridaya* or the Centre of one's being, which is like the centre of a wheel, where all the spokes meet, resides that Supreme Being. Meditate on that Supreme Being as the Self, as *aum*.

Previously, *aum* was mentioned as being used to reach the target. Here, the target is shown – it is in "the inner heart." It need not necessarily mean the physical heart; it could mean the Centre of our being. Whenever you say "me", you point towards your heart. So, fix your attention there at that Centre, from which everything proceeds and where everything goes back. Consider yourself as *aum* and meditate on that aum as self, so that you move far from darkness.

SHLOKA 7

yah sarvajnah sarvavid yasyaisha mahimaa bhuvi
divye brahmapure hy esha vyomny aatma pratishtitah

"He, who is all-knowing; He, who is all-wise; to whom belongs this greatness of the earth, sitting in the divine city of Brahmaa, in the ether of the heart, is that Self established."

The all-knowing, all-wise Brahman, because of whom the entire glory of the earth is, resides in the divine city of the heart. He is Self-established. Nobody needs to establish Him. He is *swayambhu* and also *swayam pratishtita.* And, as the *rishi* said earlier, "Meditate on that Being as *aum.*"

The Upanishad goes on describing this in different ways, looking at it from different angles.

SHLOKA 8

manomayah praana shareera netaa
pratishtitonne hridayam sannidhaaya
tad vijinaanena paripashyanti dheeraah
aanandaroopam amritam yad vibhaati

manomayah praana shareera netaa – "He consists of the mind; He is the one who leads; who is the leader of life and body…"

pratishthita anne – "…and as the nourisher of everything, he sits as food…"

"He consists of the mind; He is the one who leads; who is the leader of life and body and is seated as food." Now *annam* need not necessarily mean the food that we eat. It means "the nourisher". He is the nourisher of the entire system.

And what does He do? "He sits, controlling the heart" – *hridayam sannidhaaya.* Till now, *hridaya* had not been mentioned; only terms like "center", "inner", "secret" were used. Only now, for the first time, "heart", *hridayam,* is mentioned.

hridayam sannidhaaya tadvijnaanena paripashyanti dheerah
aanandaroopam amritam yadvibhaati

When He withdraws, we are dead. This not only applies to the microcosm which is the body; it also applies to the macrocosm, the cosmos. He is in the heart of the cosmos, the Centre of the cosmos. He is in the microcosm, if you consider the human body as a small world, with the arteries and veins like rivers; and the bones as the mountains, as it was described earlier. There, He sits in the *hridaya sthana* as the Supreme Being, nourishing and controlling everything.

When He is seen, He is first to be seen "within" and then He is seen "without". You cannot first see Him "without" – you can only find Him "within" first. And when He is seen "within", He is also seen "without". That is why I have mentioned the microcosm and the macrocosm.

SHLOKA 9

bhidyate hridayagranthih
chidyante sarvasamshayaah
ksheeyante chaasya karmaani
tasmin drishte paraavare

What happens when the Supreme Being is seen in the lower and the higher? *bhidyate hridayagranthih chidyante sarvasamshayaah* – "the knot of ignorance is cut asunder." No more can such a Being be conditioned to think, "This is mine." His world has expanded. He is not anymore revolving around just himself. There are people, who talk very high philosophy, but try taking a small thing away from them and for ten days, they are worried about it. "How I loved my pen. Who has taken it? Where is it gone?" This is because the idea of possession has not gone. Such a person's philosophy is not experiential but is theoretical.

Here we are talking about a Being who has understood the Reality seated in the heart; who has understood that it is "here" and also "there". For such a person, the "knot of ignorance", which means "that which conditions one and says, this is mine and that is yours", is cut asunder. Then all the doubts are dispelled. Doubts generally arise because I am conditioned to think that I am a separate entity from the other. "I must get this and if I do not get this, then ...", "Maybe he is telling the truth, maybe not..." – all these doubts cease because one is no more functioning in the field of thought, in the field of the brain. Once the "knot of ignorance" has been cut asunder, one has suddenly become free. All doubts are dispelled and his deeds terminate. He does not have to do anything to see that Supreme Being. He has realised that he is himself, in essence, That Supreme Being – the "higher", as well as the "lower".

SHLOKA 10

hiranmaye pare koshe
virajam brahma nishkalam
tacchubhram jyotishaam jyotih
tad yad aatmavido viduh

"In the highest golden sheath is Brahman without stain, without parts, pure, the light of lights – that is what the knowers of the Self discover."

What do the knowers of the Self discover? *hiranmaye pare koshe virajam brahma nishkalam* – "In that golden sheath is the *Brahman,* without stain and also without parts.""In the highest golden sheath" – this is a way of expressing that It is the highest because gold has always been regarded as the most precious of metals. It is "with no parts" – there is no diversity; thus It is one absolute unity. And it is that Supreme Being without any *kalanka,* "without any stain" – *nishkalam* (pure).

It is the "light of lights", *jyotishaam jyotih,* brighter than any light that you can conceive of.

"That is what the knowers of the Self know" – *tad yad aatmavido viduh.* They see It as shining brighter than the brightest in the *hridaya,* "heart".

SHLOKA 11

na tatra sooryo bhaati na chandrataarakam
nemaa vidyuto bhaanti kutoyam agnih
tam eva bhaantam anubhaati sarvam
tasya bhaasaa sarvam idam vibhaati

"Where the sun does not shine" – There is no need for sunlight. This "light" is not the light that we know of. This is the "inner light", "the light of inner effulgence" – *bhaati.* So there is no need of the sun to light That. In fact, the sun derives its capacity for lighting from that Supreme Self. So the sun shines not there. It does not mean that we enter some dark cave where Brahman sits. "The lightning also does not shine there" – *nemaa vidyuto bhaanti.*

If all that does not shine there, the *rishi* asks, *kutoyam agnih,* "How will the fire – *agni* – light?"

That means that there is no fire there to light It as It is not a material object. It is not that which is illumined by the material sun, or that which is cooled by the material moon, or that which is lit up by the stars, like the night skies, nor is It that which needs fire, to be visible.

tam eva bhaantam anubhaati sarvam – "Everything shines only after that primeval 'light'." That "light" shines and due to that everything else also shines. It is not as if you can find It with a torch – It is the "battery" that lights the torch itself.

It is like the "eye" that sees everything. The eye cannot see itself but that does not disprove its existence because without it, we cannot see anything else.

tasya bhaasaa sarvam idam vibhaati – "His shining light illumines all this world." All that shines here shines because of His shining – let us put it that way.

When I was a young boy, I used to go to a Christian missionary school. I read the Old Testament a couple of times and I found a very peculiar statement, which used to worry me; but I believed in it, of course. It said, "In the beginning, God said, 'Let there be light', and there was light." And after a long time, God created the heaven and the earth and then he made the sun and the stars. I used to wonder how there could be light when the sun and the stars had not yet been created! That which was mentioned as the "light" there, perhaps, was not the light of the sun, but the "spiritual light" or "the effulgent light". God said, "Let there be light and there was light", is a very cryptic yet simple way of putting it. There is no other way in which you can describe It.

In fact, there are many parallels: St. John, for instance says, "In the beginning was the Word and the Word was with God and the

Word was God." You can find, roughly, the same statement in the RigVeda:

prajapati vai idam agre asit
tasya vaak divitya asit
vaak vai parabrahma

"In the beginning was Prajapati, the Brahma; from Him proceeded the Word and that Word itself is that Supreme Reality."

In the beginning was the Word, the *pranava,* "the original sound". Therefore, to get to that Supreme Being, it is also possible to proceed through the *pranava,* because that is the first sound that has come out of It.

"Where the sun shines not, nor the moon, nor the stars, nor the lightning, nor fire – but everything shines only after that primeval Light. His Light illumines this entire world."

SHLOKA 12

brahmaivedam amritam purastaad brahma
paschaat brahma dakshinataschottarena
adhaschordhvam cha prasritam
brahmaivedam vishvamidam varishhtam

"That Supreme Being, Brahman, is verily this immortal Being, Brahman. In front is Brahman, behind is Brahman, to the right and to the left. It spreads forth below and above. Brahman indeed is this universe." That means, wherever you look you can only see Brahman.

In fact, the Chaandogya Upanishad says, *sarvam kalvidam brahma* – "All this is the Supreme Being." But the way we look at it, we think that it is not.

"Brahman indeed is this universe" – *bramaivedam vishvam idam varishtham.* It is the greatest. There is nothing greater than that. That Supreme Being is this Brahman and this, what we see, is also that

Brahman. There is no way that Brahman can be separated and it is that highest Brahman, wherever we look.

Therefore, you are free to find your own definition for It – call It, "God". But then, if that is the Supreme, all-pervading God, It has to be here, there and everywhere! This is one way of saying, "It is up, down, below, on all sides – surrounding everything!" There is no place where you can look and you cannot see the Supreme Being.

I am reminded of an old story of how Guru Nanak was once sleeping at a place with his feet towards the direction where people usually bowed down and prayed to God. Someone came to him and said, "Please do not put your feet on that side. That is where we worship the Lord." So Guru Nanak asked him, "Look, can you show me one direction where God is not? Just one direction – so that I can put my feet there! I have to sleep and I have to put my feet somewhere. Since you say, I will put them in the other direction. But, do not forget that God is also out there! He is not only in this direction!"

Wise men may call It by different names, different directions. But the Truth Supreme is One – *ekam sat vipra bahudaa vadanti.* That *Brahman* is everywhere. It is the greatest.

Part 3: SECTION 1

In Section 1 of the third *mandala* of the Mundaka, there is a beautiful description of two birds that sit on a tree: One bird eats the sweet fruit and enjoys it and the other looks on at the bird that is eating and enjoying. So, think of two beautiful birds sitting, on the same branch of a tree – one is eating the fruit and the other is just watching, without eating.

It is a description of beauty and also a wonderful example because the *rishi* makes a comparison between the bird who is eating and the person who is immersed in grief, who is deluded by his sorrows. When he sees the other, who is sitting quietly, without experiencing these things, he becomes free from sorrow! We will not go into it now. I am only giving the example. Make what you will of it!

This is the beauty of the Upanishad. One would think that the Upanishad is discussing the highest metaphysical truths – but then, one finds it coming down to such a simple and practical example that what seems like the flight of metaphysical fancy, suddenly comes down to something we can understand and grasp.

The Upanishads are excellent writings. But they took on the written form only much later. In fact, the Upanishads first saw the light of the world outside India because of Dara Shikoh, one of the brothers of Aurangzeb, who was a great Krishna *bhakta*. He translated the principal Upanishads into Persian and Arabic for the first time, sometime around 1600. That was the time when the Arabs traveled a lot and they carried the Upanishadic translations with them; at least the *sufis* did (those who delved into the inner understanding of Islam). And, it went to Greece or *Yunaan*; in Arabic, Greece is called *Yunaan*. That is why Arabic medicine is called *Yunaani* medicine. As the Arabs travelled extensively, they took something from here and put it there; they brought something from there and put it here.

Then in Greek, Upanishad was translated as "Upanikhat" roughly around 1760. It was when it was translated into Greek that the world began to understand what wonderful teachings these were, so ancient and yet so fresh, applicable to any time, to anybody!

In fact, the first English translation of the Upanishad came very late – sometime in the 1800's. The first person to translate the Upanishad into English was Raja Ram Mohan Roy. Max Muller translated it after him and then came various others like Sir Monur Williams, who compiled a Sanskrit-English dictionary. So the whole thing went to the West and when it went to the West, we woke up and said, "Ah! What wonderful teaching!" Till then, we had little idea about it! Of course, those who knew did know.

There is an interesting little incident from Sri Ramakrishna Paramahamsa's life. One day, a man came to him and said, "The Bhagavad Gita is a beautiful scripture – it has to be read!" Ramakrishna turned to another person near him and said, "I have been telling this gentleman for the past one year, to read the Gita. Today, some Englishman must have told him the same. So he says, 'It's a wonderful book'!" These things happen. Swami Vivekananda walked around this country with barely any food to eat, in rags. There was hardly anybody who listened to him in those days. When he went West, they recognised him and then he was recognised here! There is a beautiful address recorded when he reached Calcutta and the entire public of Calcutta went to receive him. He reprimanded them saying, "What were you all doing when I was walking around here?"

There is a story of a *sufi* teacher who had a disciple, who, for twenty-five years, wandered around with him. The disciple was quite dejected as he had not achieved that supreme peace which everybody seeks.

One day, while they were going for a walk, he asked the master, "Sir, I have been with you for twenty-five years now. Here and there I have experienced certain things – but, where is the abiding peace and the merging with the Supreme Being, which you speak of?"

The master kept quiet, because sometimes it is wiser to keep quiet than to talk. He then said, "Come on, walk with me!" They went to a riverbank and the master walked into the river and the disciple followed him. They went almost neck deep. When the disciple was beginning to wonder what was going to happen, the master caught his head and pushed it under the water and held down there. The disciple struggled with all his might. But the master was very strong and he continued to hold him down.

The disciple, in his last moments, thought, "What kind of a master is this? You ask him a serious question and he is trying to drown you!" When he could no longer struggle for that last gasp of breath, the master let go! So out came his head! And then they walked out.

The disciple asked, "Sir, what was this that you were doing to me?"

The master said, "When your head was inside the water, at that last minute before I let go, how much did you yearn for a single whiff of oxygen, fresh air?"

The disciple said, "Sir, with all my life!"

The master said, "When your desire for the Supreme Being would become as intense, then the Supreme Being would have been found already!"

Often, our aspirations are not so keen and so we try to invent various excuses – there is nothing wrong in that! If we could at least admit it, it is okay. We need not all suddenly become *satyakaama*! What we normally do is to get a little bit of satisfaction here, a little bit there. We want to have everything, and religion too, like a rose, is worn in the lapel. If we are happy, that is fine – it is better than nothing at all! But, when the urge to know the Supreme becomes very serious, when that becomes the priority, the path opens up!

*****

This Upanishad is indeed wonderful! Here is the description of two birds sitting on a tree. It talks of the sublime and suddenly comes down to mundane things, which we see and understand.

SHLOKA 1

dvaa suparnaa sayujaa sakhaayaa
samaanam vriksham parishasvajaate
tayor anyah pippalam svaadv atty
anashnann anyo abhichaakashiiti

"There are two birds – companions, always together. They do not go separately."

tayor anyah pippalam svaadv atty – "Of these two, one eats the sweet fruit..." *pippalam* means "sweet fruit", not a *peepul* tree or a *peepul* fruit.

"...the other looks on, without eating."

There is a great deal of depth in this. Basically, it means that the *atman,* or the Self, is the Witness to everything that is happening; all the activities, actions and states of consciousness of the mind. The mind, the ego enjoys; and since it enjoys, it also suffers.

There is no enjoyment without some degree of suffering in it. If you want to get any enjoyment, you have to work hard. Working hard is a suffering. You work hard because you want to enjoy. That working hard is a fact, but the hardness is forgotten as the mind is fixed on the aim of attaining joy.

The ego, which is one bird, eats and enjoys and also suffers. The *atman*, the Self, which is the other bird, sitting on the same branch, is the one that witnesses all this. It is linked to that mind, but It neither eats nor suffers but It enjoys all that is happening by just watching the enjoyment. And that *atman* is "a spark" from "the blazing fire," which is the *paramaatman*, the Supreme Being.

There is a further description:

SHLOKA 2

samaane vrikshe purusho nimagno
aneeshayaa shochati muhyamaanah
jushtam yadaa pashyaty anyam eesham
asya mahimaanam iti veetashokah

"On the same tree, a person, a *purusha*, immersed in sorrow and deluded, grieves on account of his helplessness, but when he sees the other bird, the worshipful Lord and His greatness, he becomes free from sorrow!"

According to the Upanishad, the sorrow of birth and death, the sorrow and the misery of the external world are felt only as long as one is identified with the ego. The sorrow ends the moment one realises that one is the other bird, really speaking, which is the Witness of all that is happening, which is a "spark" of the Supreme Being. We will not get into the argument now whether it is "a spark" or "the whole". Let us say, "spark" – at least qualitatively, it is the same. So when that identification is gained, then all this misery vanishes because one knows that one is not the bird which is eating, but the bird that is watching.

There is another interpretation for this. On the same tree, sit the two birds; one is eating the fruit and the other is not. Actually, if one could identify oneself with that Supreme Being, one can eat and still remain without being affected by the sorrows, which means that one realises that the eating is as imaginary as a dream. When you are in a dream-state, if there is a tiger running behind you, you run with all your might because you do not know when the tiger is going to pounce on you. In fact, it is so real, that even when you wake up, you are still sweating and feel palpitation of the heart. After you wake up, you say, "Oh! It was a dream!" and you realise that there was no real tiger.

In the same way, in the waking-state, the identification is wrong. It is not the actual person, but the identification. As long as one is identified with the bird that is eating, then there is all the misery and the suffering, and also the enjoyment within. But when one wakes up from the dream, the identification itself is lost. One realises that there is no such bird that was eating – there is only one bird sitting and watching; although, from the relative point of view there are two birds.

When one realises one's true identity as a "spark" of the Divine, as opposed to the limited ego which enjoys and suffers, then one becomes "free from sorrow" – *veetashokah.* There is no more *shoka* for such a person; there is no more sorrow.

SHLOKA 3

yadaa pashyah pashyate rukmavarnam
kartaaram eesham purusham brahmayonim
tadaa vidvaan punyapaape vidhooya
niranjanah paramam saamyam upaiti

"When the seer sees that golden, shining, effulgent Supreme Being" – who is the Witness of all the activities that go on, but is not affected by the activities – "who is also the Source of everything, including Brahma, the creator, of golden hue" – then, being the Knower and not the known, shaking off good and evil and free from any kind of stain, he attains supreme equality with the Lord.

That means, when the true identity of being that "spark" of the Supreme Being is discovered and one attains that supreme state, when one is no longer identified with the temporary ego, then one becomes free from stain, free from good and evil.

"Free from good and evil" needs some explanation. "Free from good and evil" means one is no longer being identified with the ego. It is the ego which has good and evil. That Supreme Being, that "spark" of the Divine, is equally present in the good as well as the evil; but to find It, you have to first shift from evil to good. Once found, there is no difference between good and evil for the one who has found It.

But, for the one who has not found It and is still trying to find It, there is still the differentiation between good and evil. One cannot dump everything all at once and say, "I'll do what I like; there is no good or evil – I am the Supreme Being!" It could be dangerous! One of the reasons why the Upanishads were not discussed in public was because they could very easily be misconstrued and misinterpreted and used as an argument for living as one likes: "There is no good, no evil – so what?"

The people who ask us to do *sadhana* are not fools! One can approach *satva* only by first shifting from *tamoguna* to *rajoguna* and then to *satvaguna*. You cannot remain in *tamoguna* and say, "I am free." Only when one has reached the *satvikguna* can one become *gunaateeta*. You cannot suddenly jump from *tamoguna* and become free from all *gunas*!

SHLOKA 4

praano hy esha yah sarvabhootair vibhaati
vijaanan vidvaan bhavate naativaadee
aatma kreeda aatmaratih kriyaavaan
esha brahma vidaam varishthah

praano hy esha yah sarvabhootaamvibhaati – "Truly, it is the Light that shines forth in all beings." It is very beautifully put. No being can be removed from the Light that shines forth. From the point of view of one who has reached the highest Reality, there is no thing or person who can be called, "bad".

vijaanan vidvaan bhavate naativaadee – "Knowing this, the wise man does not talk of anything else." The "wise man" – the *vidvaan* – who has understood that Brahman, never says something is "bad" or "evil" because he sees it is the same Light that shines forth in all beings. He does not see what they are doing. He sees only that Light which shines forth in all beings. Therefore, he does not talk about anything else. When he sees a person, he does not say, "He is a horrible person." He says, "He is one of the 'sparks' of that 'light.' It is veiled for the time being but it will be unveiled, eventually."

aatmakreeda aatmaratihkriyavaan esha brahmavidaam varishthah – "Sporting in the Self, enjoying the bliss of the inner Self, he works. He is great among the knowers of the Brahman." Knowing this and sporting in the effulgence and unlimited bliss of the inner Self, delighting in the Self, he works. In this sentence is the word, *kriyaavaan,* "doing work". This is to prove that such a person, who is established in the Supreme Being, who is enjoying the bliss of the Supreme Being, does not shut himself up in a room. He works; he is a *kriyaavaan*. How does he work? He works without any selfish motive, and working without any selfish motive, he has tremendous energies generated because the energies are not dissipated by success, failure, depression, exultation and so on. In that tranquility, the access to the Supreme Energy is tremendous.

Great people and saints like Shankaracharya, Madhvacharya and Swami Vivekananda, in the recent past, have done tremendous work in a few years of their lives, which a hundred people cannot do in a hundred years. You sometimes wonder how, in their short span of life, they could have done all those things that they did. But they worked, not for themselves, but for a certain cause. They worked with the understanding that *praano hy esha yah sarva bhootaam* – "That all beings are part of that Supreme *praanah*, that Energy."

The Upanishad says, such a person is a *kriyaavaan*. He is not a man who has stopped all actions. On the other hand, he is full of action. But that action is a different kind of action.

The Ishaavaasya Upanishad makes a statement:

kurvann eveha karmaani jijivishec chatam samaah – "You can do your *karmas* for a hundred years..."

evam tyayi nanyatheto asti – "that is the only way you can exist..."

na karma lipyate nare – "without allowing the impurities of the stains of *karma* to touch you."

You can perform your *karmas* for a hundred years and yet be free. How? If you would only understand what we said earlier that is the *shloka* with which the Ishaavasya Upanishad begins:

ishaa vaasyam idam sarvam
yat kincha jagatyaam jagat
tena tyaktena bhunjeetha
maa gridhah kasya svid dhanam

Here too, *karma* is mentioned. The Upanishad does not say, "Do not do any *karma*." It says, "If you live with the understanding that *ishaa vaasyam idam sarvam*", that Supreme Being pervades everything here; just as it is said in this Upanishad that, *praano hy esha yah sarva bhootair vibhaati* (That *praana*, that Life-energy pervades everything here), then one can "Let go and rejoice!" – *tena tyaktena bhunjiitha.* Normally we associate enjoyment with acquiring, hanging on to, grasping. Here is an Upanishad which says, "Let go and rejoice!" because everything is that Supreme Being and you are part of that Supreme Being. Therefore, all this is immersed in eternal joy!

If you live like that, *kurvann eveha karmaani jijivishec chatam samaah* – "You can work for one hundred years without the stain of *karma* sticking on you."

It is the same as that is said here. The one who works with the understanding that the Supreme Being is his true essence, *esha brahma-vidaam varishthah* – "Such a one is the greatest of the knowers of Brahman."

SHLOKA 5

satyena labhyas tapasaa hy esha aatmaa
samyagjnaanena brahmacharyena nityam

antahshareere jyotirmayo hi shubhro
yam pashyanti yatayah ksheenadoshaah

How does one attain that Being which is, by nature Light, which is within the body? You can attain It by *satya tapasya brahmacharya samyagjnaana* – "It can be attained by truth, austerity and sacrifice, chastity, right knowledge."

This Supreme Self within the body, the Supreme Being which lives within the body, which is of the nature of Light, which is pure, is attained by "truth".

Working towards It, not worrying about the consequences is "austerity". "Austerity" need not necessarily mean to have only one loincloth. It means, working towards that Supreme Being, no matter what the consequences.

It can be attained through "right knowledge" and with the constant practice of "chastity". Now, "chastity" means "chastity in thought, word and deed". "Chastity" means no falsehood of any kind. *Brahmacharya* means those activities that take you towards Brahman. It also includes control of the sense organs of course; otherwise, the sense organs will run away with you! What it means is that you should be in control of your sense organs, not that the sense organs control you.

If these four are followed, says the Upanishad, then that Supreme Being can be attained. The great ascetics, the great *yogis,* the great meditators, with all their imperfections gone by constantly working towards It, behold the Supreme Being, who is, after all, our own inner Self that lives within the body.

Now we come to something, a part of which has been framed and hung in all our government offices and administrative power centres.

SHLOKA 6

satyameva jayate naanritam
satyena panthaa vitato devayaanah
yenaakramanty arishayo hy aaptakaamaa
yatra tat satyasya paramam nidhaanam

satyameva jayate naanritam – "Truth alone wins, not untruth."

satyena panthaa vitato devayaanah – "By truth is laid out the path leading to the Gods."

yenaakramanty arishayo hy aaptakaamaa

yatra tat satyasya paramam nidhaanam – "...on which the *rishis,* the great sages who have their desires fulfilled, travel, to the supreme abode of Truth."

One must note: "Truth alone conquers, not untruth. This alone is the path, which leads one to that abode of the Supreme, on which the *rishis* have traveled." What kind of *rishis*? Those *rishis,* who have had their desires fulfilled, travel on the path.

There are two meanings to this: One is that when one reaches there, all one's desires are fulfilled because, after all, one seeks happiness and there, one comes to that which is the Essence of all happiness. The other meaning is that unless one's ordinary desires are fulfilled to some extent, one finds it difficult to travel along the path because, while one is traveling, these little desires hinder one from moving forward.

That is why in the normal course of things, it is better for a person to go from the stage of a student to that of a family man and then go to *sanyasa*, rather than head straight to *sanyasa*. It is possible, perhaps, for one in a million, but not generally. If these little desires are fulfilled, one may begin to see the futility of fulfilling them; that there is nothing much – even the donkeys fulfil some of these basic desires!

Seeing that, and "letting go" of it, one goes further up. One travels on the path and reaches that Supreme Abode, "not through untruth, but by truth" – *satyemeva jayate naanritam.*

SHLOKA 7

brihaccha tad divyam achintyaroopam
sookshmaaccha tat sookshmataram vibhaati

dooraat sudoore tad ihaantike cha
pashyatsv ihaiva nihitam guhaayaam

"The Supreme Being is vast, divine, of unthinkable form…" – no amount of our thinking can describe that Supreme Being.

sookshmaaccha tat sookshmataram – "It is subtler than the subtlest…"

vibhaati – "It shines forth…"

How does it shine forth? *dooraat sudoore tad ihaantika* – "Farther than the far, yet near at hand, It shines forth." We think that It is far, yet, It is near, which means that It is all-pervading. It can be here, It can be there, at the same time.

And where does It sit? "It sits in the secret place, as seen by the intelligence." Those who have understood It, can see that It resides "in the secret place", very much in the heart. You do not have to search for It anywhere else.

There is another religious book in which this is described as, "That Supreme Lord is nearer to you than your own jugular vein!" It has been described as "vast, unthinkable" and so on. We would wonder if we can ever find It? They say, "Do not search outside; It is right here inside!" Kabir has said *moko kahan dhundhe re bande mai toh tere paas hun.* "Where are you searching for me, my dear? I am right here before you, in you, near you."

SHLOKA 8

nachaksushaa grihyate naapi vaachaa
naanyair devaistapasaa karmanaa vaa
jnaana prasaadena vishuddhasattvas
tatas tu tam pashyate nishkalam dhyaayamaanah

"He is not grasped by the eye, nor by speech, nor by other sense organs, nor by austerity, nor by work" – none of these things can go near that Supreme Being. When one's nature is purified by the light of knowledge, then He is seen in meditation. When the mind has become purified, when the nature has become purified, then He is seen – not through austerity, not through rituals – all these are necessary to purify the nature. If one's nature is not getting purified, then they are futile, because unless the mind is clear and pure and stainless, He cannot be seen.

In the New Testament, there is a lovely saying in the 'Sermon on the Mount': "Blessed are the pure in heart for they shall see God." So that is what is essential. However much knowledge we have, it is not enough; purity of heart is essential to see Him.

SHLOKA 9

eshonur aatmaa chetasaa veditavyo
yasmin praanah panchadhaa samvivesha
praanaischittam sarvamotam prajaanaam
yasmin vishuddhe vibhavaty esha aatma

"That subtle Self, that *sookshma* Self, is to be known by the quiet mind in which the senses, in five different forms, are centred."

That Self is to be known or understood by the mind, from which all the five senses derive their nourishment. In fact, the senses are moving towards enjoyment. There is no sense that does not move towards enjoyment. This search for happiness of the senses is really a search for the Source from which they have started. At the back of the mind, the mind knows that somewhere, there is happiness, which is permanent. But it searches for it in the wrong direction, through the senses. The moment it realises that there is very limited happiness that can be derived by the senses, it moves back and gets to the Source from where it started, which is inside. And then, it experiences bliss.

Man's entire thought is pervaded by the Self. "When thought is purified, the Self shines forth."

So the mind cannot find the Supreme Being basically because it is always engaged in the satisfaction of the senses. The moment it realises the futility of it, then it quietens down. No more does it try to satisfy itself through the senses. When the mind becomes utterly quiet and still, when there is "purification of thought"; then the "Self shines forth" not before that!

SHLOKA 10

yam yam lokam manasaa samvibhaati
vishuddhasattvah kaamayate yaamscha kaamaan
tam tam lokam jaayate taamscha kaamaams
tasmaad aatmajnam hy archayed bhootikaamah

"Whatever world a man with purified nature desires, that he attains. Therefore, let him who desires prosperity, worship the knower of the Self."

We were talking about the Self and now, we also talk about "the knower of the Self". What a man of purified nature thinks of, in his mind, that he acquires. That is because his mind, which is purified, is not agitated by the "happenings" in the world around him. It remains calm and tranquil, free from agitation and therefore, free from dissipation of energy that normally takes place with a disturbed mind. His energies are all gathered and are complete and concentrated. When such a person fixes his mind on doing something, he definitely achieves it, because it is for the good of the world – it cannot be for himself.

If a person, who has sworn to tell the truth even at the cost of his life, practices *satyameva jayate,* then *satyam* really wins and conquers untruth. Even if, by mistake, he utters something wrong, that will also turn into the truth! In the same way, when a man of purified nature, who remains calm, collected and tranquil and does not let his senses agitate him, fixes his mind on something, he definitely attains it. So the *rishi* says, "Therefore, if you desire prosperity, worship the knower of the Self." Now "prosperity" here need not mean material prosperity alone. Anyone who desires prosperity and cannot worship that Supreme Being, must at least worship "the knower of the Self".

By worshipping and understanding or living with "the knower of the Self", you will also attain that calmness and tranquility of mind by which you will also be able to attain your desire. But, by then, by the end of the day, living with such a person, your only desire will be to attain *moksha*; because you will see how happy this person is, not bothered about anything else. So, why go for anything else?

Part 3: SECTION 2

SHLOKA 1

sa vedaitat paramam brahma dhaama
yatra vishvam nihitam bhaati shubhram
upaasate purusham ye hy akaamaas te
shukram etad ativartanti dheeraah

"He who knows that Supreme Abode of Brahman, wherein the world shines brightly, and when one is established there, the world shines brightly."

No more is the world seen as darkness, no more is the world seen as full of misery.

SHLOKA 2

kaamaan yah kaamayate manyamaanah
sa kaamabhir jaayate tatra tatra
paryaapta kaamasya kritaatmanas tu
ihaiva sarve pravileeyanti kaamaah

"He who entertains desires, thinking of them all the time, is born here on account of his desires." If I desire something with my entire mind and I cannot attain it in this life, then, according to the Upanishadic or Vedic theory, I will attain it in some other life – in the next, perhaps.

"But in the case of a wise man whose desires have ended, who has realised the Self, all desires vanish right here, in this life."

Desires are entertained in the mind. Thus, to control the mind is the first step. It is easier said than done! Arjuna tells Krishna, in the Gita, "Krishna, my mind is very difficult to control. It is stronger than the wind. I try my best, but very often, doubts trouble me. What will happen to such a person like me, who has left the shore of this world and has not yet reached the other shore? I am in-between!" This is the state of *yoga brashta* or "fallen from yoga".

Krishna assures Arjuna that whatever one builds up spiritually in this life, will be counted from where one has left off, in the next. We do not have to go back to square one! Krishna says there is a possibility of two kinds of birth that one may take, which will give a good start: one may be born either in a very affluent and good family or in a family of *yogis*.

One may be born in an affluent and good-natured family, so that very soon in life, one not only sees all the desires fulfilled but also sees the futility of fulfilling them and so gives them up and moves towards the path. Or one is born in a family of pure *yogis,* who are not bothered about their material welfare at all, so that from childhood, one is turned in that direction. The latter is rare.

So, he who has desires is born here on account of his desires. But the one who has his desires fully satisfied realises that all joys lie in understanding the Supreme Being – for such a perfected soul, all desires vanish right here on earth! He does not have to come back again and again.

SHLOKA 3

naayam aatmaa pravachanena labhyo
na medhayaa na bahunaa shrutena
yam evaisha vrinute tena labhyas
tasyaisha aatmaa vivrinute tanoom svaam

naayamaatmaa pravachanena labhyo na medhayaa na bahunaa shrutena – "This *atma,* this Supreme Brahman cannot be attained by instructions, nor by intellectual power nor through much hearing." All these are important but you cannot achieve that Supreme Being by any of these ways. Then how does one attain Him?

yamevaisha vrinute tena labhyastasyaisha aatmaa vivrinute tanum svaam – "He is to be attained by the one who is chosen by the Self! To such a one, the Self reveals His own nature."

That means, do not think that you can achieve the Supreme Self by gate-crashing the Supreme Self. First, realise your limits, realise the limitations of your intellectual powers. You cannot find It through instructions, through *pravachana*. You cannot understand It by your intelligence. If you are proud of your intelligence and think you can understand the Supreme Being by sitting down and working on your computer, no, you cannot! Nor can you find It through much hearing. If you have heard the Upanishads a thousand times, you may not still have understood the Supreme Being.

Then, who can know Him? "He is understood by him who is chosen by the Self." One interpretation to this is that all *sadhana* and all effort towards the understanding of the Supreme Being, is to the extent of purifying the mind, clearing all the obstacles – that's all! Up to that extent, one can go. After that, any attempt to superimpose the experience of the Supreme Being, ends up in imagining that one has reached the Supreme Being. After that, what does one do? One has to settle down quietly, relax and wait patiently for the Supreme Being to reveal Itself.

It is like cleaning up the room, dusting the carpet, opening the doors and windows and then sitting down, waiting for the breeze to blow – you cannot command the breeze to blow. And, when the breeze blows, if your windows are shut, it will not come in! So, all your activities, all your *sadhana*, all your knowledge, is "the opening of the windows". It is very essential. But, you cannot make the breeze blow. The breeze will certainly blow – it has blown before and it will blow in the future. You have to wait. You cannot choose when it should happen.

Therefore, there are a few guidelines to be followed. The Upanishad itself declares, "He who says he knows, does not know; and he who says he does not know, knows." That means, once It is known, the ego cannot sit up and say, "I have known It!" This is because It is known when the ego has disappeared. And any attempt to try to forcibly dissolve the ego, generally ends up in strengthening it. So that is where the question of patience, surrender and faith arises.

What I am trying to explain is what the Upanishad intends to explain; that the search for *moksha* is not a career to be pursued. It is to be done with the utmost humility, with the understanding that one needs to dissolve one's centre. You cannot attain the Supreme Being by sitting down and doing controlled breathing a few times every day. If that was the case, then it would have been very simple – hundreds of people would have attained the Supreme Being!

All that effort and *sadhana* is necessary to purify your mind, to keep your windows and door open. The grace has to come. It is like the lovely breeze that comes in. But then, the room has to be clean – that is *sadhana*. Otherwise, the breeze will bring in the dust.

The other interpretation to the statement "He is to be attained by the one, who is chosen by the Self", is that it means that the Supreme Being is realised by him alone whose only aim is to find the Supreme Being – nothing else is his priority!

SHLOKA 4

naayam aatmaa balaheenena labhyo
na cha pramaadaat tapaso vaapy alingaat
etair upaayair yatate yas tu vidvaams
tasyaisha aatmaa vishate brahmadhaama

Having said that we cannot reach It and that we have to depend on the grace of the Supreme Being to attain It, the *rishi* says that it does not mean that you must become weak and give up and say, "I am not going to struggle." He says, *naayam aatmaa balaheenena labhya* – "This Self cannot be attained by one without strength." So, full-fledged attention and complete dedication to the understanding of the Truth is essential.

This Self cannot be attained without strength nor through heedlessness: "Let the Self reveal Itself – I don't care!' Such heedlessness will not help; nor does austerity without an aim. Austerity is fine, but the aim of austerity must be to find the Supreme Truth. I may say, "I am a very austere and simple man." But that simplicity may be for convenience – and may have nothing to do with finding the Truth. If I have four pairs of *khaddar* dresses, it is very easy for me to maintain them; It does not mean I am austere. So, austerity with an aim is required; not austerity without aim.

"But he who strives by these means…" What are the means? "Through strength, through austerity with an aim…", and being perfectly heedful of what he is doing – "…enters the abode of that Supreme Brahman."

What is the nature of the liberation that takes place in this manner?

SHLOKA 5

vedaanta vijnaana sunischitaarthah
sannyaasa yogaad yatayah shuddhasattvaah
te brahmalokeshu paraantakaale paraamritaah
parimuchyanti sarve

"The seers, rishis who have discovered and understood well the meaning of the Vedanta knowledge, who have purified their nature through renunciation, dwell in the world of Brahma and are all liberated at the end of time, being one with the immortal."

SHLOKA 6

sampraapyainam rishayo jnaanatriptaah
kritaatmaano veetaraagaah prashaantaah
te sarvagam sarvatah praapya dheera
yuktaatmanah sarvam evaavishanti

"Having attained Him, those seers, those *rishis* who are satisfied with their knowledge of the Supreme Being; perfected souls, who are free from passion and are tranquil; having attained to that omnipresent Self on all sides, they, with concentrated minds, enter into that *sarvam*, into 'That, which is everywhere' and become one with It."

SHLOKA 7

gataah kalaah panchadasha pratishthaa
devaascha sarve pratidevataasu
karmaani vijnaanamayascha aatmaa
parevyaye sarva ekeebhavanti

What happens when one enters the *sarvam*? "Gone are the fifteen parts with their supports…" That means all that supports the sense organs, all that supports the *tatvas*; everything goes back to its Source.

"…and all the Gods enter into their corresponding deities", meaning, all the sense organs go back to their Source. The "senses" are the "Gods" and Indra is the "chief God of the senses" – that is why they are called *indriyas*. All the senses go to their Source – no more are they indulgent.

"One's deeds and the Self consisting of our understanding – all have become one with that Supreme Being." So all that started from "the blazing fire" has now gone back into the central Source – let's put it that way.

How has it all gone back?

SHLOKA 8

yathaa nadyah syandamaanaah samudre
astam gacchanti naamaroope vihaaya
tathaa vidvaan naamaroopaad vimuktah
paraatparam purusham upaiti divyam

"Just as the flowing rivers disappear into the ocean, casting off names and shapes, even so the knower of that Supreme Being is freed from name and shape." No more is the knower known by his name, or his shape or his form – "He attains to that Divine Person, higher than the high!"

SHLOKA 9

sa yo ha vai tat paramam brahma veda
brahmaiva bhavati naasyaabrahmavit kule bhavati
tarati shokam tarati paapmaanam
guhaagranthibhyo vimuktomrito bhavati

"He who knows that Supreme Brahman becomes Brahman Himself." No more does his ego bother him, it is finished! He has identified himself with that Supreme Being.

"In his family, no one who does not know the Brahman will be born. He crosses over sorrow, he crosses over sins, liberated from the 'knot of the secret place', he becomes immortal." Liberated from the "knot of the heart", liberated from the conditioning of his individual soul, he becomes immortal!

It is interesting that "In his family no one who does not know the Brahman will be born." Now, two things have to be clarified – one is that I do not think it applies to children who were born before he realised Brahman. The other is that even if the knower of Brahman has a child, do not judge the child only by the present birth – perhaps he would be a knower of Brahman at some point earlier.

SHLOKA 10

tad etat richaabhyuktam
kriyaavantah shrotriyaa brahmanishthaah
svayam juhvata ekarshim shraddhayantah
teshaam evaitaam brahmavidyaam vadeta
shirovratam vidhivad yais tu chirnam

This is the doctrine declared in the *Rig* verses: "Those who perform the rites, those who are learned in the scriptures, who are well established in Brahman, who offer of themselves oblations to the Sole

Seer, with faith, to them alone should one declare this knowledge of Brahman."

"By whom the 'rite on the head' has been performed, according to rule, this knowledge of Brahman is to be given…" Do not throw around this knowledge and waste it. Offer it only to those who perform the rites of the journey, who have, with great faith, learned the scriptures to understand the Supreme Truth; who are well-established in the service of Brahman, who are in search of Brahman, who offer themselves as oblations to that Sole Seer, with faith; who have performed the "rite on the head". That means those who have performed the rite of total surrender to the Supreme Being, to the Truth.

"Rite on the head has been variously interpreted. Some people interpret it as one who has shaven his head, tonsured his head and so on, which is also, actually, an external symbol of completely surrendering oneself to the Truth. Only to such a one whose first priority is to understand that Supreme Truth, may this doctrine be given – this is declared in the verse – not to one who is unfit.

SHLOKA 11

tad etat satyam rishir angiraah purovaacha
naitadacheernavrato dheete
namah paramarishibhyo
namah paramarishibhyah

tad etat satyam – "This is the Truth." The seer, the Rishi Angirasa, declared it before: "Let none who has not performed the ritual, which we have mentioned before, study this. Salutations to the great seers! Salutations to the great seers, the *rishis*!"

This is how the Mundaka Upanishad ends.

One should not think that we are trying to become exclusive by saying that we should not give it to others. What the *rishi* is trying to say is that it is futile to study all this, unless one's priority is to find the Truth.

Of course, none of us are searching for the untruth. But then, the Upanishadic teaching is that the Truth is, "That which when known, everything else is known." So, search for That! That is why it is studied, to try to understand It. But the practice of it can come only when one's priority is to find that Truth; otherwise, one can have endless discussions on the subject, but return to where one started. As it is said in the Rubaiyat of Omar Khayyam, "Coming out through the same door through which one went in."

Aum shantih shantih shantihi!

www.ingramcontent.com/pod-product-compliance
Ingram Content Group UK Ltd.
Pitfield, Milton Keynes, MK11 3LW, UK
UKHW021702190726
13853UKWH00001B/400

9 788195 608942